contents

Introduction

Something surprising is happening with aprons.

They're breaking out of the kitchen and demanding to be recognized as a fashion statement. Here's what I mean: I recently saw a stylish young thing waiting at a bus stop. Her razored haircut was the bomb, and she had on a chic top, skinny jeans—and a crisp craft apron. I'm not used to seeing aprons out in public, so I asked her about it. She told me she wears it all the time; the pockets are handy for holding keys, money, ID, and stuff. She looked down at the pretty fabric and slid her finger along some ribbon trim. "And it's *awfully* cute!" she exclaimed.

And she was so right—it was totally cute. And so are the aprons I'm seeing more and more. The little accessory that once symbolized a dreary kind of domesticity has had a massive makeover. Now made in curve-hugging shapes and sassy prints, aprons can also be embellished to die for. They're not there to catch gravy stains anymore, sister! They've been liberated from function and elevated to an art form.

You've probably seen aprons popping up in upscale catalogs and hip discount stores (you know which ones I mean). But if you're the DIY type—and I bet you are—the great thing about aprons is how quick and easy they are to sew. I'm probably partial, but this book contains 25 of the prettiest aprons ever, plus templates and instructions for making them. The styles cover the entire gamut, from bibs to smocks to craft aprons. Some are flirty and ruffled, others straight and no-nonsense, but *all* are delightful. The luxe Marie Antoinette (page 84) is a fancy confection perfect for hosting a dressy party. The Lorelei (page 65) evokes sassy, gum-snapping waitresses in '50s diners. Stitched in a playful cotton print, the versatile Dig It (page 37) has plenty of pockets, perfect for tucking gardening tools and just the thing for stuffing supplies while crafting. With its playful mix of fabrics, pom-pom trim, and rickrack edging, the Cakeland (page 40) makes it clear it's time for fun.

A Is for Apron

25 Fresh & Flirty Designs

Nathalie Mornu

LARK BOOKS

A Division of Sterling Publishing Co., Inc.
New York / London

Art Director
Dana Irwin

Cover Designer
Cindy LaBreacht

Photographer
John Widman

Illustrators
Amy Saidens *figurative*
Bernadette Wolf *instructional*
Orrin Lundgren *templates*

Library of Congress Cataloging-in-Publication Data

Mornu, Nathalie.
  A is for apron : 25 fresh & flirty designs / by Nathalie Mornu
      p. cm.
  Includes index.
  ISBN-13: 978-1-60059-201-0 (hc-plc with jacket : alk. paper)
  ISBN-10: 1-60059-201-5 (hc-plc with jacket : alk. paper)
  1. Aprons–Design. 2. Sewing. 3. Tailoring–Patterns. I. Title.
  TT546.5.M67 2008
  646.4'8–dc22

                                                          2007038057

10 9 8 7 6 5 4

Published by Lark Books, A Division of
Sterling Publishing Co., Inc.
387 Park Avenue South, New York, NY 10016

©2008, Lark Books

Distributed in Canada by Sterling Publishing,
c/o Canadian Manda Group, 165 Dufferin Street
Toronto, Ontario, Canada M6K 3H6

Distributed in the United Kingdom by GMC Distribution Services,
Castle Place, 166 High Street, Lewes, East Sussex, England BN7 1XU

Distributed in Australia by Capricorn Link (Australia) Pty Ltd.,
P.O. Box 704, Windsor, NSW 2756 Australia

The written instructions, photographs, designs, patterns, and projects in this volume are intended for the personal use of the reader and may be reproduced for that purpose only. Any other use, especially commercial use, is forbidden under law without written permission of the copyright holder.

Every effort has been made to ensure that all the information in this book is accurate. However, due to differing conditions, tools, and individual skills, the publisher cannot be responsible for any injuries, losses, and other damages that may result from the use of the information in this book.

If you have questions or comments about this book, please contact:
Lark Books
67 Broadway
Asheville, NC 28801
828-253-0467

Manufactured in China

ISBN 13: 978-1-60059-201-0
ISBN 10: 1-60059-201-5

For information about custom editions, special sales, premium and corporate purchases, please contact
Sterling Special Sales Department at 800-805-5489 or specialsales@sterlingpub.com.

The best part: unlike stitching pants or a shirt, you don't have to worry about fit—making an apron the perfect project for a beginner. This book assumes you already have some basic sewing skills, that you have a handle on laying out patterns and understand terms like topstitching and right side versus wrong side. You don't have to be an expert on all things sewing, though. A section in the front covers techniques you may not have tried yet, like stitching yo-yos, making your own bias tape, and mitering corners.

In the back, you'll find a bonus section of ideas for embellishing commercial aprons or transforming something you have lying around into an apron. Most of these can be done in no time flat. Busy schedules don't always allow for fabric shopping, cutting and pinning, and stitching and hemming. If you have friends coming over for book club in an hour, check out this part of the book, and you can wow them with the teeny-tiny tartlets you whipped up *and* with your sewing skills.

Finally, because I can't get enough aprons, the book includes a six-page gallery of vintage aprons, each sweeter than the last. As I admire them, I can't help but wonder about the women who once tied them on. When I put on an apron, I feel transformed. The apron seems to channel everyone who's ever worn one before. I'm suddenly more efficient, more in charge, and totally up to the task before me—doesn't matter if it's pulling weeds from my herb garden or entertaining a dozen friends gathered to celebrate a birthday.

Long live the apron! It's been emancipated from drudgery. Just as our title says, *A Is for Apron*—and for adorable, awesome, amazing, attractive, appealing, and most important, *awfully* cute.

anatomy of an Apron

aprons have been around almost forever—the Bible, in fact, reports that Adam and Eve fashioned aprons from fig leaves. And while Neolithic bloggers didn't exist to confirm this, cave dwellers cooking near open fires must have placed something across their laps for protection. The point is, no one can say for sure when the first apron was invented, but it's a safe bet that five minutes after Grog sewed the last stitch through a flint-knapping apron made of saber-tooth tiger hide, Ogga said, "Ooh, I like the ties behind the neck! I want one just like it, but add something to hold berries and stuff. By the way, what do you call that thing?"

Since Ogga's time, we've come up with several types of aprons—not to mention words to describe all the styles and parts. Here's what you'll find today.

These days, **bib aprons** abound. Simple to make, easy on all body types, and offering a lot of protection up where the action is, they hang from the neck by straps or a loop connected to a "bib" that covers the chest. Bib aprons reach to mid-thigh, the knee, or lower. Picture a barbeque apron, and chances are you've got the classic bib in mind.

Half or waist aprons—think June Cleaver—have no bib, and tie with two straps at the back or around the back to the front. Their skirts can be flat in a variety of shapes, such as gored or pleated, or simply a large rectangle with ties. Like its bibbed cousin, the half or waist apron comes in various lengths right down to the ankle. This is the ultimate all-purpose apron to wear around the kitchen while fixing easy meals. And if you're giving a party, tie on a pretty waist apron and get out where it's happening. Care for a canapé with that martini?

Cobbler aprons cover both the front and back of the upper body. They fasten on with waistbands at the back, or with ties at the sides. Remember the cafeteria ladies from school? Little did you realize their aprons descend from the medieval tabards worn by knights. These babies are true workhorses. If you're rolling up your sleeves to work with clay, glue, paint, hot water, bleach, wallpaper paste, and more, it wouldn't hurt to suit up in the "armor" afforded by a cobbler.

With **smocks**, you have no strings attached, literally. These close relatives of cobbler aprons are loose, coat-like garments with short or long sleeves, or none at all. They can be pulled on over the head or buttoned up the front or back for the greatest amount of coverage. If you envision a granny in a housecoat, think again—smocks are hot! They look great paired with the latest jeans and boots, or you can wear them as summer dresses showing lots of shapely leg. They're comfortable, too. If you're a mom-to-be, you probably have at least one.

Those are the styles. Now let's run through the parts.

THE FRONT OF AN APRON includes the skirt, and the bib if you're making that type. Since the front uses most of the fabric, consider its shape before you choose your material. Fronts can be single-sided or reversible, overskirted, gored, pleated, gathered, or flat and unshaped, just to list a few possibilities.

bib

skirt

pocket

hemline

tie

You've come a long way, baby

Then...

A farmer's wife gathered eggs in it

NOW
Gather compliments on your cute fashion accessory

Then...

An apron was handy for shooing away flies

NOW
Use one to shoo your friends through the door for a girls' night out

Then...

In a pinch, it wiped the dust off a sideboard

NOW
Tie one on to spiff up an outfit that's got you bored

Then...

Wives wore pretty but bland aprons when entertaining hubby's boss

NOW
Wear a saucy, spicy, sexy apron while entertaining a date

Then...

Deep pockets held clothespins galore for hanging laundry

NOW
Deep, oh-so-stylish pockets hold your cell phone, TV remote, and iPod

9

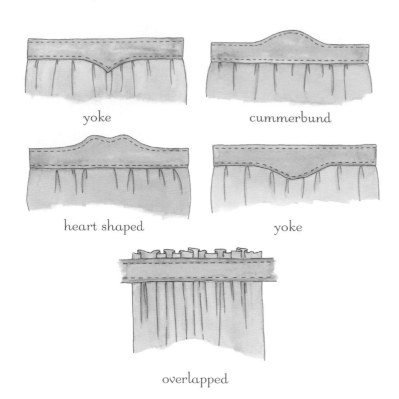

yoke

cummerbund

heart shaped

yoke

overlapped

WAISTBANDS ARE OPTIONAL depending on the design. Not all aprons have a waistband, but when they do, they can be a separate piece or made from the same strip of fabric as the ties or sashes. Make the waistband tall or short to suit your body shape and the apron design. Sew it up in the same fabric as the front or in another fabric that contrasts and frames the front with energy and style.

TIES COME NEXT, unless you're making a smock or a pinafore. Sashes might be wide, or narrow strings, or anything in between. You can make them super-long and wrap them around to tie in the front. Wide ties can be pleated where they attach to the waistband, or matched exactly to the waistband's width. Point the tips, square them off, or invert a point in the ends—whatever strikes your fancy. You can decorate tie tips with lace, a contrasting fabric, or add some bling with beads and sequins. Before you determine how wide to make the ties, think about the bow they'll form. A sassy bow in back speaks volumes!

Moving down, HEMLINE DESIGNS ADD PERSONAL-ITY and dash. Cut them straight or scalloped. Round them off or make them pear-shaped. Pipe the edges; add any number of embellishments including ribbon, ruffles, and patchwork; or simply fold back a crisp mitered hem and be done.

FINALLY, THE POCKETS. Not all aprons have them, which begs the question...why not? With all due respect to utility—and to Ogga—pockets are a very cool design element. They can define your apron faster than anything else, except maybe the fabric you use. Want to emphasize a shapely hip or saucy fabric? Add one, two, or even more pockets. While you're at it, put the ruler down and vary the shapes. Round, oval, heart-shaped, gathered, even pockets on pockets.

Think, too, about pocket locations. This is your apron; make it work for you. Customize the hand entry: If you're a southpaw, mounting a pocket on your right hip makes no sense. Put your hand where you want that pocket to be—there's nothing worse than a pocket too high, too low, or too far behind you. And unless you're adding a pocket for pure decoration (well, why not?), make it big enough to do its job.

Before you begin, consider how to attach the pockets. Patch style or in seam? Whether you decide to hide those pockets or flaunt them, it's smart to reinforce the top corners so all the things you stuff inside don't cause them to rip away from the apron. Otherwise, you'll end up with torn-up, grunge-rocker aprons.

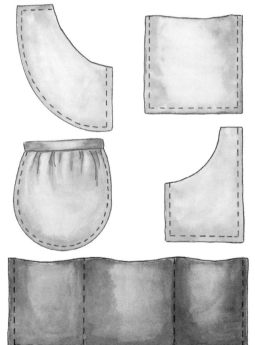

Whether you're making pasta from scratch, firing up the grill, sculpting a life-size bust for your gallery opening, or sponge-painting a Tuscan dining room, you want a good-looking apron between you and your activity. But do you have to look like Granny Clampett while you wear it? Nope. As this book shows, aprons today are all about style and attitude. So you won't find a pattern for Ogga's apron in this book. On the other hand, Eve's fig leaf concoction does have possibilities...but I'll leave that up to you.

Conventional pockets, like these, are nice, but feel free to get adventurous with the shapes.

Getting Started

*a*fter you select one of the projects and begin to design your own apron, remember: it's all about mix-n-match. The style possibilities, shape variations, and what you choose to insert or leave out—that's what makes designing and wearing aprons so much fun.

Supplies

To create a fabulous apron, clear off a table or some floor space and round up the necessary tools (page 14). Set up your sewing machine, ironing board and iron, and you're almost good to go. All you need are a few basic supplies.

Material World

Every part of stitching aprons is fun, but the first pleasure comes in choosing the fabric. Fabrics appropriate for aprons run a wide and colorful gamut, but consider a few things before making a selection. For aprons that will receive heavy wear and use, machine washable and dryable cloth is best—stay away from fabric that requires special cleaning and care. If you're partial to totally natural fibers, go for it, but be forewarned—you may be chained to the ironing board to keep that 100% cotton or rayon apron from looking like a dust rag. Poly-cotton blends spell zero pressing, but if you're making an apron for kitchen use, keep in mind food stains, especially oils, can be hard to remove from synthetics.

Take a stroll through your favorite fabric store and let your design sense and preferences guide you. Talk with clerks and don't overlook the drapery section and remnant tables—some beautiful aprons have emerged from those departments.

Ruffles, Ribbon, and Rickrack

Thinking of embellishing your apron? That's a no-brainer: of course you are. I don't know about you, but when I'm in the trims department, I can barely contain my squeals of delight. Next time you're there, visualize rickrack and ribbon running along edges and framing pockets, emphasizing the structure of the apron. Picture cording wandering across the apron skirt in quirky designs. Think about finishing your apron with a row of pre-made ruffles. Do you fancy yourself eyelash-batting girly? Whoever said less is more was deeply mistaken! Frou-frou the edge with three, four, five rows of ruffles. Speaking of feminine, get some lace. It can enhance pockets, a hem, or completely cover waistbands and ties. And lace bows—oh, be still my heart.

Consider the entire apron as a canvas. And remember: decorative touches don't only come by the yard. Think buttons where you wouldn't ordinarily use buttons—attach them in a circle or on the top of a bib as a monogram, for example. Or sew on charms that echo an apron's style and fabric designs. Why not add a full quilt block smack dab on the apron front, or appliqué a strip of patchwork anywhere you like—near the hem, at the waistband, even on the ties? Apply yo-yos for little puffed fabric counterpoints (learn how to make these on page 20). Add beads, sequins, and iron-on patches. Or dive deeper into handwork and embellish with embroidery and cross-stitch. Fabric paint is lots of fun and not just for kids! Ditto stenciled designs. And while you're having fun, tack on tiny action figures from the local toy shop or attach a tiny pocket for your iPod nano, and...well, you get the point.

Feeling Biased

If you're not feeling especially ornamental or don't have a ton of time, pick up some bias tape, because when it comes to finishing your apron, this stuff can be a godsend. It's ready-made, gives you an impeccable edge, and frames the apron nicely. It comes in a couple of different widths so you can choose what you like. You'll find standard black and white, as well as a large selection of solid colors to match or contrast with your print. Since bias tape colors tend to follow fabric color trends, what you find in shops will most likely work with most of the bolts in stores. If you want to spice up edges with a print rather than a solid color, as was done on Fruit Tart (page 52), it's a simple matter to make your own bias tape. (See page 18 for instructions.)

It's a
material
thing

Lead-lined rip-stop nylon
X-ray technicians

Rubber
Nursery-workers, florists

Leather
Blacksmiths, cobblers, woodcarvers, dog trainers

Oilcloth or rubberized canvas
Commercial fishers

Heavy canvas
Mechanics, painters, military gunners

Vinyl or plastic
Pet groomers, dishwashers, jewelry makers

Mixing + Matching Fabrics with

flair

basic apron styles haven't changed much over the years; it's the fabrics you choose that make an apron uniquely yours. Unless you want to look like a traveler at the retro depot—and I'm not saying that's a bad thing— mix it up.

You don't have to follow the color rules you've learned. For example, tastemakers used to say complementary colors (those on opposite sides of a color wheel) clashed. Pshaw...nobody believes that anymore. Yellow and purple look great together. Try other unexpected combinations that make a bold statement—pair scarlet and lime green, for example, or hot pink and orange.

How about tipping the scale? For drama, team a large print with a small, inconspicuous one. All you need is color to tie the two fabrics together. While you're messing with proportions, stitch a huge pocket on a tiny apron, as was done on Deep Pockets (page 55) and Dig it (page 37).

Loosen up by mixing materials you wouldn't usually associate. Silks with wool suiting, tulle with denim, velvet with hints of burlap. Why not? Rough textures juxtaposed with soft ones look so interesting. I also love combining mismatched period prints; again, it's all about using color to link the patterns together. A formal jacquard looks really interesting when contrasted with something modern.

If you feel timid about doing this kind of thing, just start small, by using unexpected trims. And if you need a little dose of courage, remember you can use binding tape to draw all the elements together.

Other Material Considerations

What else will make your apron a work of art? Lightweight fusible interfacing keeps a waistband from wrinkling into an accordion while you're wearing it. Good quality thread and fabric always add to the life of your apron—so buy the highest quality you can afford.

Finally, if you decide to use vintage fabrics, especially if you want to mix them with new fabric, consider lining the vintage pieces so they can support and tolerate the same use and wear as the newer fibers. Even so, it's still a good idea to hand-wash the apron to preserve its life.

Tools and Equipment

With the exception of a sewing machine and a quality pair of shears, the tools you need to make an apron are low-cost and in nearly every sewing basket. See the Apron Kit on the next page for a list of what's really handy to have.

One thing that will make an immeasurable difference in your sewing experience is a large work surface. Sure, you can pretzel yourself on a clean floor, but working at a height where you can stand and walk around easily makes everything sooo much easier. If nothing else, clear the mail, magazines, and other junk off your dining table and work on it, but consider buying a cutting mat to protect it from scissor gouges and other damage.

Speaking of cutting mats, fabric shops and stores that sell quilting and crafting supplies carry these. Anyone with a rotary cutter already has a mat, and probably a straight-edge, too, but you don't need to go out and stock up on any of these

Apron Kit

You only need a few basic tools to make aprons, and even if you're a novice sewer, you probably already own almost of them.

Shears Typically a bit larger than scissors, high-quality dressmaker's shears have razor-sharp edges and a heft that makes cutting fabric a breeze. Never cut anything but fabric with them. Ever.

Scissors Keep a couple pairs on hand, one for trimming fabric and thread and—since paper dulls blades—a cheap pair for cutting out patterns and anything besides cloth.

Thread, pins, and needles For professional results, don't scrimp on quality with these, especially if you're working with delicate fabric.

Tape measure For accuracy, use one that doesn't stretch.

Sewing machine It's fine if your sewing machine makes nothing but straight stitches and zigzag, but machines with fancy embroidery stitches give you extra options for embellishments.

Iron and ironing board Use a sturdy padded ironing board and a steam iron.

Water-soluble fabric pens These pens make blue lines that disappear when you mist or dab them with water. Don't iron over them first or they could become permanent.

Transfer pencils Some sewers use transfer pencils to trace an embroidery design onto paper and then hot iron the design directly onto fabric. If you're low tech, however, you can always use the window method (page 22).

things if you don't already own them. While they're great for cutting straight lines, for the projects in this book shears will work just fine.

This covers the supplies you'll need. If you want to check out a few particular techniques I use, turn the page. Or if you can't wait to get started, skip ahead and refer to the Techniques section when you need to.

Techniques

aprons are pretty simple to make and perfect projects for a new sewer. Do note, if you don't already know how to sew, this book will not teach you how. You should already be aware of fabric grain and know how to lay out patterns, cut out fabric pieces, operate a sewing machine, and understand basic sewing terminology such as "topstitch" and "seam allowance."

Enlarging the Templates

You can enlarge the templates in the back of this book using a photocopier. If you're like me—too busy and (I'll be honest here) mathematically challenged—go to a place that offers large-format copying or take the book to a business that provides reprographic services, which means they print blueprints. It's so much simpler for the staff to scan the patterns, enlarge them in a few easy keystrokes, and print them on large sheets. Full-service copy shops can usually enlarge the templates for you, too; take that route if you don't mind taping several sheets of paper together.

Seam Allowances

Unless it's noted otherwise, the aprons in this book have seam allowances of ½ inch (1.3 cm).

Finishing Seams

If you wear your apron for more than show, it's going to go through a lot of washing and drying.

This causes raw fabric edges to unravel, so finish all exposed seams or you'll end up with an ugly, frayed mess. Your choices for finishing include pinking, zigzagging, serging (if you've got a machine), or even la-de-da fancy French seams. Sure, it takes a little extra time, and it feels like a drag when you're in a hurry to get to the good part—the sewing. Hey, if you're okay with dangling dreadlocks of matted thread, you can skip this step.

Pressing

When sewing, you should press rather than iron. In pressing, you place the iron where you want it, give a little blast of steam to open up seams, then lift the iron and set it down again in a new area. In contrast, when ironing, the iron gets pulled across the fabric to smooth out wrinkles; this can stretch the fabric, and you don't want that. After pressing, pause a few seconds to let the piece cool before picking it up so the fabric doesn't stretch.

Pleating the Ties

You can create wide apron ties and then pleat them at the point where they attach to the waistband or apron front. Fold the fabric into one or two pleats—whatever you like—pin, then baste, making sure the basting stitches are parallel to the raw edge (figure 1). Press to flatten and make it easier to stitch it to the waistband.

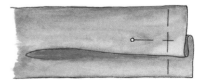

figure 1

In a Bind: Sewing on Bias Tape

About a third of the aprons in this book are edged with bias binding. Here's how to apply either pre-packaged double-fold bias tape or bias strips you've made yourself (page 18). *Note:* The difference between ¼-inch (6 mm) double-fold bias tape and ½-inch (1.3 cm) single-fold is a pressing matter, literally. If you purchased single-fold bias tape, fold the strip in half lengthwise and press it to get ¼ inch (6 mm) double-fold tape, which is the width I recommend you use to bind an apron. (To make it clearer what's going on, all the illustrations except figure 5 show the binding beginning at the corner of the fabric, but when lapping ends, you should not start at a corner.)

1. Begin by sewing a row of stay-stitching ¼ inch (6 mm) away from all the raw edges to bind. Trim back the seam allowance so that only ⅛ inch (3 mm) remains beyond the line of stay stitching.

2. Measure the distance to bind, add 5 inches (12.7 cm), and cut this length of binding strip. With the folds in the tape facing away from the apron, pin one raw edge of the binding to the raw edge of the wrong side of the apron. Stitch around the edge in the crease of the tape (figure 2). Stop stitching 3 inches (7.6 cm) from the starting point and clip the loose end so that 1 inch (2.5 cm) of tape overlaps the part that's sewed down.

3. Flip the bias tape to the right side of the apron, fold the raw edge of the tape under, and pin it down, as shown in figure 3. Machine stitch near the fold of the bias tape (figure 4), stopping 2 inches (5.1 cm) from the starting point.

4. To tidy up the ends, lap them by folding the loose tail under ½ inch (1.3 cm), as shown in figure 5. Finish stitching the binding down.

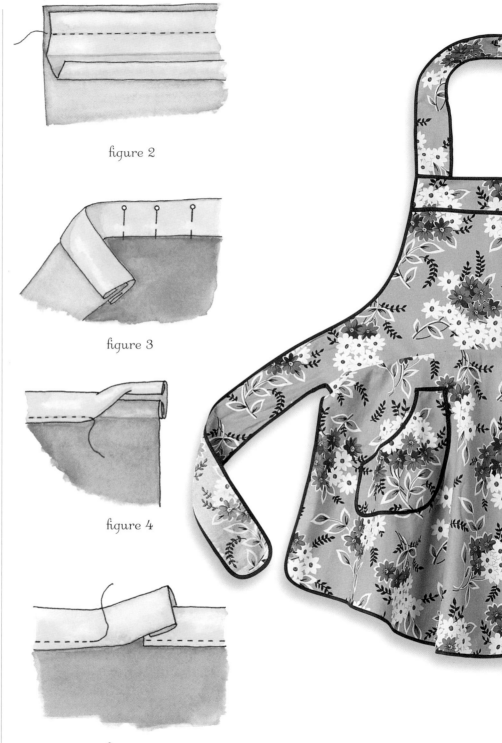

figure 2

figure 3

figure 4

figure 5

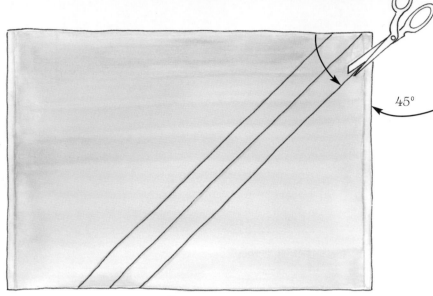

figure 6

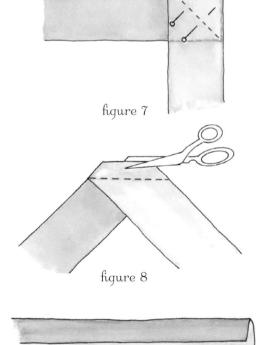

figure 7

figure 8

figure 9

Making Cool Bias Tape

Purchased bias tape is like a TV dinner—cheap and convenient, but ultimately kind of bland. Add spice by making your own bias tape. To give the appearance of perfect harmony with the apron's personality, use the same fabric as for the apron or a solid color that's a flawless match rather than a close one. To really pump up the flavor, cut bias tape from a complementary print. It only takes a few minutes and makes an apron really pop.

1. Cut strips four times as wide as your desired tape at lines running 45° to the selvage (figure 6). You'll need enough strips to create a band that, once stitched together, can cover the circumference of the apron plus some extra.

2. Place one strip over another at a right angle with the right sides together. Stitch diagonally from one corner to the next of the overlapping squares (figure 7).

3. Snip off the corners along the seam, leaving a ¼-inch (6 mm) seam allowance (figure 8). Open up the seams, and press the allowances flat. Repeat steps 2 and 3 with all the strips to make one long piece.

4. Fold the strip in half lengthwise, right side out, and press. Open the strip, and press the raw edges into the center. Now you have single-fold bias tape (figure 9).

To make double-fold bias tape, fold again in the center and press, as shown in figure 10.

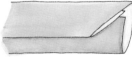

figure 10

Inserting Rickrack in Seams

Add a splash of fun to pockets or to lines of stitching by sewing rickrack into the seams.

1. Position the rickrack on the right side of the fabric so the "humps" along one side are parallel with and close to the raw edge. Pin the rickrack to keep it in place. Baste along the center of the rickrack using big stitches (figure 11).

2. Measure the distance between the edge of the fabric and the center line of the rickrack; this will be the seam allowance. Pin the piece of fabric and the element you wish to stitch it to, right sides together, and sew, using the determined seam allowance. When you turn the pieces right side out, you'll find the rickrack, sandwiched between, with only half of the humps showing.

figure 11

fit to be tied

One size fits most with the aprons in this book, but if you're concerned, you can make a muslin sample first. Obviously, you can easily alter aprons made of rectangular pieces (such as those on pages 37, 80, and 93) by simply extending or reducing the width. Other aprons in this book can be slightly adjusted by altering the percentage by which you enlarge the templates. Other than this, it can be fairly complex to alter size considerably. While the front may fit, for example, the neck ties may not end up in the right place. If you're confident you know how to alter, have at it. Otherwise, leave it to a pro.

Making Yo-yos

Charming and whimsical, these puffy little rosettes are fun to make and add a sweet accent. They're so easy to whip up that you'll want to embellish not just aprons but purses, coats, blouses, quilts... They can also be garnished with a bead or a button, as shown on Grape Swirl (page 96).

1. On a piece of cardboard, draw a circle twice the size of the desired yo-yo plus another ½ inch (1.3 cm) for seam allowance. Cut it out. Using a fabric marker, trace one circle per yo-yo onto cloth. Cut out the fabric along the line.

2. Fold the edge back a scant ¼ inch (6 mm) while hand sewing a running stitch close to it, using strong thread such as quilting thread (figure 13).

3. After stitching completely around the circle, gently pull the thread until the edges gather in the center, as shown in figure 14. Secure the gathers with a couple of stitches then knot and cut your thread. Squash the yo-yo flat, with the gathers centered on the top.

Flouncing Around: Making Ruffles

Need cheap frills? Gather 'round and learn how to make a ruffle.

1. Determine the depth of the ruffle and cut fabric strips at least two and a half times longer than the edge it will embellish.

2. Zigzag the raw edges to prevent fraying. Sew a narrow hem along one edge, lengthwise.

3. Sew two rows of basting stitches along the edge opposite the hem. Don't trim the thread ends; instead, pull them to gather the ruffle to the length and frilliness you want (figure 12).

4. Pin the ruffle to its base, right sides together, adjust the length and the gathers, and stitch. Et voilà!

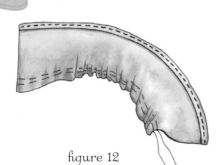

figure 12

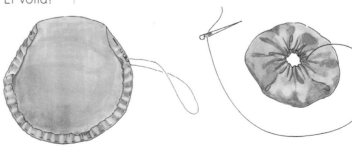

figure 13

figure 14

Hems

To create a simple ¼-inch (6 mm) hem, turn the fabric under ½ inch (1.3 cm) and press. Fold this under again by half, ending up with a double fold that's ¼ inch (6 mm) wide. Topstitch the hem on a machine, or hand-sew from the back.

Mitering Corners

Mitered corners are one of the classiest finishing techniques. The good news is they're nowhere near as difficult to make as they appear when finished. Mitering eliminates bulk and creates a tidy-looking 45° seam at the corners.

1. Press under the desired hem on each edge and then open out the folds. If you've made a double hem, open only one fold, not both. Fold the corner diagonally down to the place where the two fold lines intersect, as shown in figure 15. Note how the previous fold lines line up.

2. Press across the corner fold and check to see if you got it right by folding again along the original hemline. Your edges should now meet at a perfect angle. Cool, huh? Now unfold again and trim away excess fabric in the corner (figure 16).

3. Fold back into the mitered edge (figure 17) and slipstitch the mitered edges—the angle—together.
Victory dance!

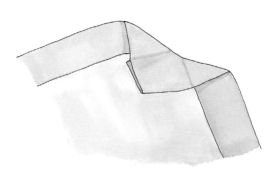

figure 15

figure 16

figure 17

Stuck on Appliqué

An appliqué is a decorative piece of fabric applied to a base cloth. By now, you've noticed the high esteem in which I hold anything decorative; true to form, I love adding appliqués as an additional level of embellishment. You can leave the edges of an appliqué raw, or turn them under.

To camouflage the stitches attaching an appliqué, poke the needle through the base fabric and up through the appliqué, right next to the fold of the turned-under edge of the fabric. Bring the needle back down into the base fabric just a wee bit away. Repeat, as shown in figure 18. When the piece is completely sewn down, take a few tiny back stitches, work the needle under the appliqué piece and across to the other side, cut close to the edge, and pull slightly. The end of the thread will disappear under the appliqué piece.

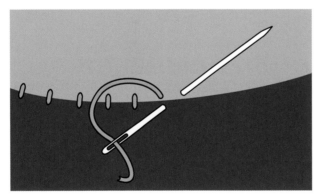

figure 18

Embroidery Primer

Here's how to embroider the stitches used on the aprons in this book. You can use as few as one or as many as six strands of floss in your needle,

depending on how fine or broad you want a design to look. You don't have to be a stickler about using embroidery needles—just pick the smallest size and type you happen to have around that holds the desired amount of floss. On the other hand, always stretch the fabric in an embroidery hoop; stitching on floppy fabric is murder.

For a beginner, it's probably easier to transfer a ready-made design to follow the lines and fill in the spaces, but confident embroiderers can do free-form stitching, as shown in Great Vine (page 113).

Transferring Designs

The low-tech method for getting a printed image onto fabric involves taping the paper on a sunny window, putting the fabric over it, and tracing the design with a water-soluble marker. That's it, no additional widgets required. Can't do without gadgets? A transfer pencil is a nifty tool for transforming any image into a pattern to embroider. You'll also need tracing paper, an iron, and an ironing board.

1. Select the design to embroider. Put the tracing paper over it, and trace firmly using the transfer pencil. Note: If you have words, numbers, or anything that will read backwards when flipped, *reverse* that part of the design before tracing it. You only have to forget this once, and you'll never do it wrong again!

2. Flip the tracing paper over, image side down on the fabric. Pin it to the cloth so it doesn't shift, and press the tracing paper with a dry iron. Presto! The image is now on the cloth. Place it in a hoop and stitch away.

Stitching

Once you master these, you can find other stitches on the Internet or in any beginning embroidery book. If needlework isn't your thing, most modern sewing machines will make some embroidery stitches, and fancy machines have entire libraries of stitches and sewn designs, computerized and ready to apply.

Running stitch Use a running stitch to outline or "draw" simple designs. Simply push the threaded needle in and out of the apron fabric, making small, even, up-and-down stitches. Take several stitches before pulling the needle completely through.

Split stitch To make a continuous, even running line, use a split stitch. Make a small stitch and bring the needle up for the next stitch through the center of the previous stitch, splitting the threads. If you make short stitches, it will resemble a slender chain stitch.

Chain stitch For a fancy outline, use a chain stitch. Bring the thread from the back to the right side of the fabric and hold it toward you with your left thumb. Take a stitch into the same hole the thread was brought through, forming a small loop. Don't pull the thread tightly. Bring the needle out a short distance forward and over the loop. Make a second loop that overlaps the first one. Repeat, creating a chain "line" as long as you want. The sidebar at right shows the entire sequence.

Satin stitch For a colorful fill of shapes and designs, use the satin stitch. Bring the thread up through the fabric and make a single straight stitch. Bring the needle out very close to the starting point of the original stitch, and plunge it back down close to its endpoint. Repeat, filling the shape with stitching. Everything should lie evenly and snugly together; it takes a little practice to get it just right.

from rags to
Stitches

Running stitch

Split stitch

Satin stitch

Chain stitch

23

Aprons— A Short and lively History

Why have people been wearing aprons for so long? The answer is necessity. Clothing fashions come and go, but aprons remain essentially the same. For most of recorded human history, ordinary people could only afford the materials and time to make a few "changes" of clothing. Really, up until about 50 years ago, most folks didn't replace clothes often or easily. They protected the ones they had. Enter the apron! While they seem humble to us today, aprons served a vital purpose through the years.

Think about it. Aprons evolved to meet the requirements of their wearers' jobs. Full-fronted, thick leather, or oiled aprons deflected sparks, animal muck, and salt water. People hauling sacks of potatoes, washing down counters, or chopping up the fatted calf wore large bibbed aprons or smocks. Lots of hard physical work? Plenty of apron!

Aprons also evolved into specialty wear. Ancient priests and Freemasons wore ceremonial aprons embellished with symbols. In fact, museums preserve the ornate Masonic aprons of George Washington and Meriwether Lewis. Folk costumes everywhere include aprons extensively decorated with embroidery, appliqué, and cutwork.

History, photos, letters, and fiction tell us that nineteenth-century mothers, aunties, grandmas, and homekeepers dried hands, wiped children's faces, dodged spattering fat, carried clothespins, picked apples, shooed cats, and fed chickens using aprons.

> After World War II, housewives had plenty of leisure to whip together stylish aprons, and they did so with a vengeance

After World War II, the rising number of household appliances and a strong economy gave middle-class American homemakers something they hadn't had much of before: free time. Housewives had plenty of leisure to whip together stylish aprons, and they did so with a vengeance. An abundance of chic apron patterns helped women

sew up themed aprons for holidays, make mother-daughter sets, and create aprons that matched their tablecloths or had coordinating hand towels or built-in potholders. After an afternoon at the sewing machine, housewives might watch TV mom June Cleaver waltz into their living rooms wearing a crisp shirtwaist, pearls, and an apron.

While aprons allowed seamstresses to show off their skills, they also served as billboards. Commercial aprons allowed women to express dissatisfaction with their roles as housewives, serving it up with a little humor. More than one apron was printed with variations on "To heck with housework!" Aprons sold then and now extol Dad's skills as a grillmaster. And as an advertising gimmick, hardware stores and other companies gave rugged canvas aprons printed with a logo, name, or specific message.

If early TV shaped a generation of wifely expectations, it also sparked a generation of feminists who wouldn't be caught dead in pearls and ruffles! And while the apron may be up front in clichés, today's women, young and old, think, "Equality? You bet! But after bringing home the bacon, I'm beat. Let's order pizza. After that, I'm going to do some finger painting with the kids. Better put on that pretty new apron I stitched up."

Courtesy of the McCall Pattern Company and of Simplicity Pattern Co, Inc.

vintage aprons

reversible
pockets a-plenty

sweet embroidery
heart-shaped waistband

unusual pocket placement
playing-card print for bridge parties

cross-stitched gingham
tall waistband, fancy hem

handkerchief apron
terry cloth

gores galore
two-tone ties

vintage aprons

scalloped hem
reversible

folkloric-style tourist souvenir
stepped hem

yoke collar, ethnic print
gathered hem

empire waist
pointed hemline

belted smock
vavoom!

delicate handkerchief hem
frilly bib

vintage aprons

crocheted
fabric pre-printed with
pattern to cut and stitch

holiday theme, trimmed with bells
pretty ruffles

Mexican smock
creative pocket

RAND FRONT — SEAM ALLOWANCE

gingham panel
applied tape detail

paper napkin stitched to grosgrain
canvas for advertisement
handkerchief apron

sawtooth hem
Asian feed sack

the projects!

amoeba

Materials

Apron kit (page 15)

Pattern (page 136)

1 yard (91.4 cm) of fabric

6 yards (5.5 m) of ¼-inch
(6 mm) double-fold bias tape

Tool

Seam leveler

I prefer classic, tailored clothing, so I seldom make frilly aprons. Never underestimate the impact of a simple design.

—Joan Hand Stroh

What You Do

1 Make a true bias fold of the fabric (figure 1, next page). Then cut out the apron using the pattern pieces on page 136. Transfer the dots from the front pattern piece onto the fabric. Don't stretch or pull the edges. Set the pieces aside.

2 Splice together the bias tape to create one long piece.

3 Bind the top edge of the apron front. Trim the binding ends even with the side edges.

4 Baste the bias tape to the ties, positioning carefully around the scallops. Press them down then sew them together, using the seam leveler if necessary. Trim the binding ends evenly across the ties.

5 Position one tie on the back side of the apron front, with the long end of the tie toward the top of the front (figure 2). Stitch close to the edge to hold the tie in place. Repeat to attach the other tie.

6 Bind the remainder of the apron front. Start on the right side, leaving about 1½ inches (3.8 cm) of bind-

ing free. Encase the edges, including the ties. Stitch around the sides and bottom of the front, mitering the corners and creating a small tuck at the bottom center of the front piece. Stitch off the end of the binding for about 1½ inches (3.8 cm).

7 Press the ties flat over the bias tape. Trim the binding end 1 inch (2.5 cm) from the top of the apron front. Fold the end under, placing it between the tie and the binding. Stitch through all thicknesses along the original stitching line.

8 Bind the top of the pocket. Trim the binding ends even with the pocket sides. Position the pocket on the skirt,

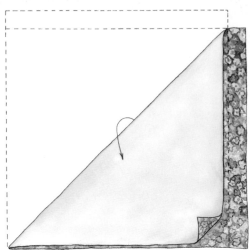

figure 1

matching the corners to the dots, and pin it in place. Fold ⅜ inch (1 cm) of the bias tape under the top right corner. Stitch the pocket in place using the seam leveler at the corners if necessary. Stop with the needle down about 2 inches (5.1 cm) away from the left pocket corner. Trim the binding to about ⅜ inch (1 cm) from the top of the pocket and finish stitching. While wearing this apron, try to be modest about all the compliments!

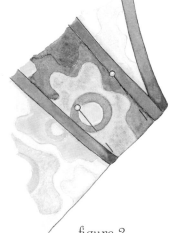

figure 2

Designer Jennifer M. Ramos

dig it

Materials

Apron kit (page 15)

½ yard (45.7 cm) of heavy cotton fabric for the front

¼ yard (22.9 cm) of another coordinating print for the pockets

½ yard (45.7 cm) of quilter's cotton for the waistband and ties

Tool

Serger (optional)

Seam allowance:
¼ inch (6 mm)
unless otherwise noted

What You Do

1 Cut all the pieces, using the schematic (figure 1) as your guide.

2 To hem the two sides and bottom of the apron front, use the serger or a zigzag stitch on a standard sewing machine. Turn in the two sides ¼ to ½ inch (6 mm to 1.3 cm), pressing them in place. Pin and hem. Do the same to the bottom then set it aside.

3 Finish all four edges of the large pocket piece by serging or another method. Turn the top edge toward the inside ½ inch (1.3 cm), press it in place, and hem it.

4 Fold the pocket into thirds, and press it again. Unfold it—the creases will serve as guides to help you determine where to divide the pockets. Fold the fabric toward the ironed crease 1 inch (2.5 cm) to the left and the right of each pressed crease (figure 2). Press and pin the folds.

5 Find the center of the apron front by folding it in half and pressing it. Open it, and center the pocket piece, right side up, on the apron front, pinning the pocket at the folds. Use as many pins as needed to keep the folds in place.

6 Turn under the two sides and bottom of the pocket's edges, again

keeping the folds in place. Press it down, and pin in place. Stitch the edges, reinforcing the stitching at the start and at the end.

7 Stitch down the valleys between the pocket folds. If you need to, pull the folds slightly apart, but don't alter the placement of the pockets. Reinforce the stitching at the beginning and end. Set it aside.

8 Turn in the top and bottom edges of the waistband piece ½ inch (1.3 cm) lengthwise toward the center of the strip. Press, fold the piece lengthwise in half, and press again. The resulting piece should look like double-fold bias tape.

9 Attach the waistband edge to the top edge of the apron front as you would apply bias tape—unfold and, right sides together, stitch along the pressed crease closest to the top edge

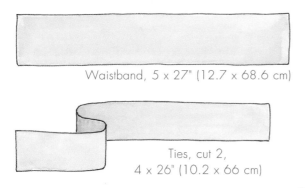

Waistband, 5 x 27" (12.7 x 68.6 cm)

Ties, cut 2,
4 x 26" (10.2 x 66 cm)

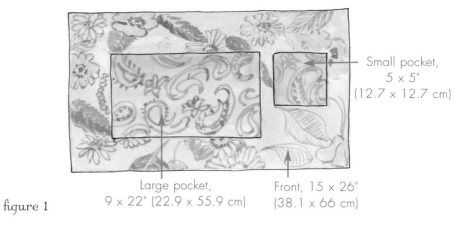

Small pocket,
5 x 5"
(12.7 x 12.7 cm)

Large pocket,
9 x 22" (22.9 x 55.9 cm)

Front, 15 x 26"
(38.1 x 66 cm)

figure 1

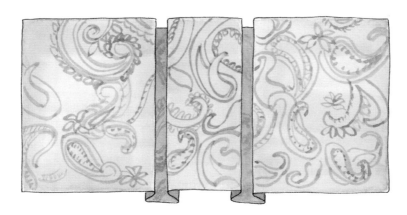

figure 2

of the apron front. Flip the apron over. With the fabric unfolded, tuck in the sides that extend beyond the apron, and press them in place. Fold the waistband over, and press it again. All the raw edges should now be concealed. Pin them in place, and sew along the bottom and top edges, leaving the sides open.

10 To create the ties, fold in one of the short edges for each tie about ½ inch (1.3 cm), and press it in place. Fold the long edges toward the inside to meet each other in the middle. Press it again. Then fold the ties in half lengthwise, so that the finished edges meet. Press, pin, and stitch in place around all three finished sides, leaving one raw, short edge.

11 Insert the raw edge of each tie into either opening of the waistband. Stitch it in place, reinforcing the stitching. Run three rows of additional stitching across the waistband, length-wise, to give it added durability. Use the sewing machine's presser foot as a guide, lining up one edge alongside the previous line of stitching.

12 Turn down the top edge of the small pocket ½ inch (1.3 cm) toward the wrong side of the fabric. Press and hem. Turn in the remaining three sides ¼ inch (6 mm), press, and hem. Pin the pocket to the side of the apron, and sew it down, reinforcing the corners with backstitching.

Cakeland

Materials

Apron kit (page 15)

Pattern (page 138)

¾ yard (68.6 cm) of fabric for the overlayer

1 yard (91.4 cm) of fabric for the underlayer

¼ yard (22.9 cm) of fabric for the waistband

¼ yard (22.9 cm) of fabric for the pocket

¼ yard (22.9 cm) of interfacing

3 yards (2.7 m) of rickrack

2½ yards (2.2 m) of ball fringe

1⅝ yards (1.5 m) of 4-inch-wide (10.2 cm) ribbon

What You Do

1 Enlarge and cut out the pattern pieces (page 138), lay them on the fabric, and transfer any placement marks. Cut them all out.

2 Using the appropriate pattern pieces, cut out interfacing for the waistband and the pocket.

3 Fuse the interfacing to the wrong side of the waistband and the pocket top edge.

4 Fold the top of the pocket over the interfacing and press. Pin the rickrack to the right side of the fabric around three sides of the pocket so that the middle of the rickrack is ¼ inch (6 mm) from the edge. Fold the rickrack to the outside, and sew it down with a ¼-inch (6 mm) seam allowance.

5 Stitch the width of the finished pocket top along both sides. Trim the corners and any extending rickrack, and then turn the pocket over to the wrong side. Fold the seam allowance along the stitching and press. When you turn the pocket to the right side, you should see the rickrack peeking from the edges. Set the pocket aside.

6 Using the overlayer, pin the top of the ball fringe to the outer edge of the right side of the fabric, and sew it down. Fold the seam allowance to the wrong side of the fabric and press. Topstitch along the seam edge you created.

7 Place the completed pocket on the indicated spot on the overlayer, and stitch it down close to the edge.

8 At the waist of the overlayer, sew gathering stitches ¼ inch (6 mm) and ⅛ inch (3 mm) from the edge, and gather evenly, using the waistband as a guide for sizing. Set the overlayer aside.

9 Follow the instructions from step 4 to attach rickrack to the underlayer. Fold the seam allowance to the wrong side of the fabric and press. Topstitch close to the edge. Then repeat step 8 for the underlayer.

10 Place the underlayer right side up on a flat surface. Place the overlayer on top, matching the waistbands. Adjust the gathers so that 1 inch (2.5 cm) of the underlayer extends out from each edge of the overlayer.

11 Pin the waistband to the two layers right sides together. Stitch them together, and then press the seam allowances toward the waistband.

12 To construct ties from the ribbon, cut two lengths 28 inches (71.1 cm) long. Fold in ½ inch (1.3 cm) from one edge, and sew it down to create a hem.

13 Gather the tie ends, and pin them to the waistband right sides together. Fold the waistband at the halfway mark, right sides together, and stitch the ends. Trim the corners as shown in figure 1.

14 Turn the ends of the waistband right side out. On the wrong side of the apron, fold the raw edge of the waistband under, and pin it over the seam, covering the stitches. On the right side, stitch close to all edges of the waistband. Cupcake, anyone?

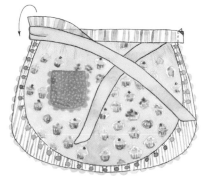

figure 1

cherry bistro

Materials

Apron kit (page 15)

Pattern (page 121)

1¼ yards (1.1 m) of cotton/
cotton blend fabric for the
apron front

⅓ yard (30.5 cm) of contrasting
fabric for the front panel

44 inches (1.1 m)
of jumbo rickrack

44 inches (1.1 m)
of medium rickrack

What You Do

1 Enlarge the pattern pieces on page 121, and cut them out of fabric.

2 To make the front panel, pin the jumbo rickrack to the contrasting fabric, 1¼ inches (3.2 cm) from each long edge. Sew two rows of stitching ¼ inch (6 mm) apart down the center of each rickrack column, removing the pins as you go. Center the medium rickrack over the jumbo, pin it, and sew.

3 Create tucks on the front panel piece by folding on the dotted line. Pin the tucks in place then baste a ⅜-inch (1 cm) seam from the top edge. Fold the rickrack over the bottom edge of the panel. Finish the outer edges and bottom with a ⅝-inch (1.6 cm) narrow hem.

4 To finish the apron front, sew a ⅝-inch (1.6 cm) narrow hem along the outer edges. Then machine stitch a 2-inch (5.1 cm) hem.

5 To make the ties, fold the fabric lengthwise in half, right sides together. Stitch one end and along the length of the tie, leaving one end open to turn it out. Trim the inside corners. Turn the tie right side out and press. Repeat to make the other tie.

" For me, the fun starts with the fabric. I come up with different color combinations and embellishments before thinking up the actual design. "

—Morgan Moore

6 Center the finished front panel on the front of the apron, and baste stitch the pieces together at the top.

7 Fold in a ⅝-inch (1.6 cm) seam allowance on both edges of the waistband. Stitch the waistband to the apron front and front panel, right sides together, ensuring that the panel is securely in the seam. Fold the waistband over, inserting the open ends of each tie (figure 1). Topstitch the ties in place and along the edge of the waistband, catching the side underneath.

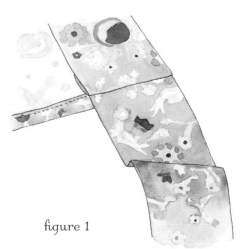

figure 1

Cosmopolitan

Materials

Apron kit (page 15)

Pattern (page 133)

1 yard (91.4 cm) of fabric

8¼ yards (7.5 m) of ¼-inch (6 mm) double-fold bias tape

2 small spools of thread

Fusible interfacing

¾-inch (1.9 cm) button

Tool

Seam leveler

> " When I waited tables, I couldn't imagine wearing what the "older" servers did, so I designed this flattering apron. "
>
> **—Joan Hand Stroh**

What You Do

1 Cut out the apron pieces using the pattern on page 133. Set them aside.

2 Splice together the packages of bias tape to create one long piece.

3 Sew the pocket linings to the lower front, wrong sides together, with a ⅝-inch (1.6 cm) seam (figure 1, next page).

4 Encase the top edges of the pocket with bias tape, stretching it slightly at the inner curve while stitching through all thicknesses. Trim the bias tape ends even with the edges.

5 Sew the pocket back to the pocket lining along the double-notched edge, right sides together (figure 2).

6 Baste the pockets to the lower front below the diamonds, then stitch ¾ inch (1.9 cm) all around the bottom curved edge (figure 3).

7 Stitch bias tape to the bottom curved edge.

8 Sew the ties to each side of the upper front piece using a ⅝-inch (1.6 cm) seam. Zigzag close to the seam, and then trim the seam. Press the seam toward the center of the upper front.

9 Sew the neck straps to the upper front piece using a ⅝-inch (1.6 cm) seam. Press the seam toward the neck straps.

10 Stitch all the way around the upper front, including the neck straps and ties, with a ¾-inch (1.9 cm) seam allowance, as shown in figure 4.

11 Mark the buttonhole on the right side of the left neck strap. Cut a rectangle of interfacing 2 x 1 inches (5.1 x 2.5 cm). Pin it to the wrong side of the fabric where you wish to make a buttonhole, but don't fuse it to the fabric. Stitch the buttonhole, then turn the fabric

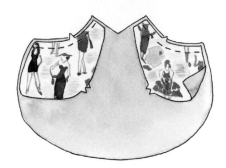

figure 1

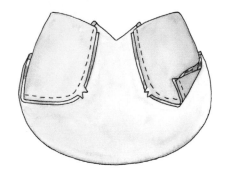

figure 2

figure 3

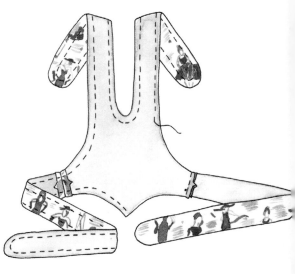

figure 4

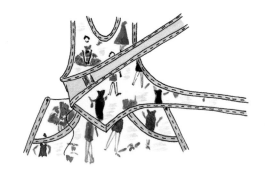

figure 5

over and trim the interfacing close to the stitching, being careful not to cut the stitching.

12 Lap the wrong side of the upper front piece onto the right side of the lower front piece, using the previously stitched placement line. Align the center lines, the sides, and the pocket dots. Baste the two pieces together (figure 5).

13 Apply bias tape to the upper front piece. Start on the left neck strap, and encase the upper front around the right neck strap, and tie. When sewing the bias tape around the outer curves of the neck strap and ties, stop before the curve with your needle in the fabric. Position the tape around the curve 1 inch (2.5 cm) at a time by hand. Gently pivot the fabric while taking five to six stitches. Stop, again with the needle down, and without raising the pressure foot, reposition the next inch (2.5 cm) of fabric, and continue on, pivoting and sewing as you go.

14 When you get to the edge where the upper front meets the lower front, stitch through all thicknesses to attach the two pieces until you get 2 inches (5.1 cm) from the center point. Stop with the needle down, and then guide the bias tape to the center point with your fingers. Miter the bias tape at the center point. Continue stitching around the apron until you've encased the entire upper front piece. Fold the trim over, and lap over the start of the bias tape.

15 Remove the stitching for the placement line. Trim the seam joining the upper front to the lower front to ½ inch (1.3 cm), being very careful not to cut the fabric underneath.

16 Cut a small square or dot of interfacing, and fuse it to the wrong side of the right neck strap where you wish to place the button. Sew the button on through the fabric and the interfacing.

46

Designer **Betsy Couzins**

lemon meringue

Materials

Apron kit (page 15)

Pattern (page 118)

¾ yard (65.6 cm) of fabric
for the front

¼ yard (22.9 cm) of fabric
for the pockets

¼ yard (22.9 cm) of fabric
for the waistband and ties

2 packages of rickrack

Interfacing

Seam allowance:
¼ inch (6 mm)
unless otherwise noted

What You Do

1 Cut out all the apron pieces according to the pattern (page 118).

2 Finish the outer edges of the front of the apron, so they won't unravel. On the right side of the fabric, place the rickrack along the outer edges with its centerline ¼ inch (6 mm) from the edge. Stitch the rickrack down the center. Fold the fabric and the rickrack under along the stitch line and press. Turn and topstitch along the fold as close to the fold line as possible.

3 As in step 2, finish the outer and inner edges of the pocket, and then attach the rickrack to the right side. Fold the fabric and the rickrack under along the stitch line and press. Turn and topstitch the inner edge of the pocket. Repeat to make a second pocket.

4 Pin the pockets, right sides up, to the right side of the apron front, aligning the notches. Stitch across the top of the pocket and around the sides, close to the rickrack.

5 Fuse the interfacing to the wrong side of the waistband. With wrong sides together, fold the waistband lengthwise down the center and press.

When I first began sewing, I made aprons because there were no sleeves or zippers to fuss with, and the result always fit. But it's astonishing how many techniques I've learned specifically from aprons.

—Betsy Couzins

6 Pin the top of the apron to the waistband, right sides together, easing it to fit and leaving ¼ inch (6 mm) of the waistband extending on either side (figure 1). Stitch, then press the seam allowances toward the waistband.

7 To create the tie, fold under the long side twice to make a ⅜-inch (1 cm) double hem. Press and stitch. To make a point, fold one end of the tie diagonally with right sides together, and then stitch it down along the long side, ⅜ inch (1 cm) from the edge. Turn the corner right side out, press, and then stitch the remaining long edge of the tie with a ⅜-inch (1 cm) double hem. Topstitch the point. Finally, create a pleat in the raw end of the tie that attaches to the apron (page 16). Repeat for the other tie.

8 With right sides together, pin the ties to the waistband, aligning the ties with the waist seam. Using the center line as a guide, fold the waistband over the ties. Stitch the ends to secure the ties (figure 2) then turn the waistband right side out.

9 On the wrong side of the front, fold the raw edge of the waistband under, and pin it over the waist seam. On the apron front, topstitch along the edges of the waistband.

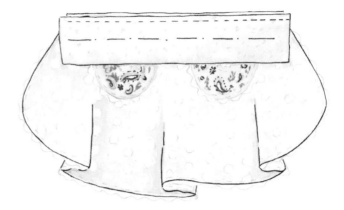

figure 1

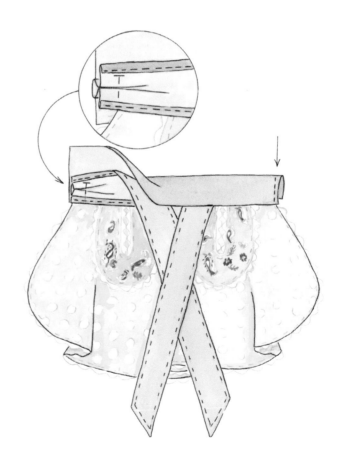

figure 2

fairy tale

Materials

Apron kit (page 15)

Pattern (page 127)

4 pieces of white cotton fabric: 2 pieces 15 x 9 inches (38.1 x 22.9 cm) and 2 pieces 8 x 4 inches (20.3 x 10.2 cm)

Embroidery hoop and needle

Embroidery floss in 10 different colors

48 inches (1.2 m) of bias tape

What You Do

1 Transfer the forest scene (page 127) to one of the large pieces of white fabric, centering it on the material. Transfer the treetop shapes to one of the smaller pieces of white fabric, leaving at least 1 inch (2.5 cm) around the edges.

2 Embroider the design according to the pattern, using any stitches you like (page 23). Fill in both treetops with fruit and leaf designs.

3 Cut both large pieces of white fabric along the exterior line of the pattern. Pin them right sides together, and sew along the curved edge, using a ¼-inch (6 mm) seam allowance. Notch the curves, turn the apron right side out, and press the seams.

4 Cut out the treetop shapes from both small pieces of white fabric (embroidered and not). With right sides facing, sew them together, leaving a 1-inch (2.5 cm) space open for turning. Turn each piece right side out, press the seams, and sew the openings shut.

5 Using the appliqué stitch (page 22), sew each piece in place on the apron, leaving the top of the shape open to form a pocket.

" Embroidery is the perfect way to illustrate a story! This apron tells of wanderings in an enchanted forest, with magic hiding just behind a tree... or in a tree pocket. "

—Aimee Ray

6 Center the bias tape along the back side of the top of the apron. Fold and iron the strip over the top of the apron. Sew the tape to the apron. Fold its ends in, and sew them shut. Give the apron to your little princess and live happily ever after.

fruit tart

Materials

Apron kit (page 15)

Pattern (page 126)

⅞ yard (80 cm) of main fabric

¾ yard (68.6 cm) of coordinating fabric to make bias tape

What You Do

1 Enlarge the pattern pieces on page 126, and cut them out of fabric.

2 Make 7 feet (2.1 m) of bias tape 2 inches (5.1 cm) wide out of the coordinating fabric (page 18).

3 Stitch the bias tape to the top edge of the pocket pattern piece.

4 Pin the wrong side of the pocket to the right side of the front, matching the bottom edges. Baste ⅛ inch (3 mm) from the bottom edge.

5 Using a water-soluble marking pen, draw a vertical line at the center of the pocket, from top to bottom. Stitch along this line to split the pocket in half, reinforcing the stitching at the top by sewing back and forth a few times.

6 Stitch bias tape around the bottom edge of the front piece, including the pocket where it's basted on.

7 Gather the top of the front evenly between the notches. Set it aside.

8 Pin two of the ties with right sides together, matching all edges. Using a ⅜-inch (1 cm) seam allowance, stitch the edges, leaving the end with the

Even taking time out to experiment, I can whip up an apron in one afternoon, start to finish. I love it!
—Nathalie Mornu

squared corners open. Trim both of the angled corners, press the seams open, and turn right side out. Press flat, and topstitch ⅛ inch (3 mm) in from the edges. Pin and baste one pleat in the center of the open end (page 16). Repeat with the remaining pieces to make the other tie.

9 Put one waistband face up on your work surface. Pin the pleated end of a tie at the center of one side, with the tie placed across the band rather than on the outside of the band (figure 1, next page). Repeat on the other side of the waistband.

figure 1

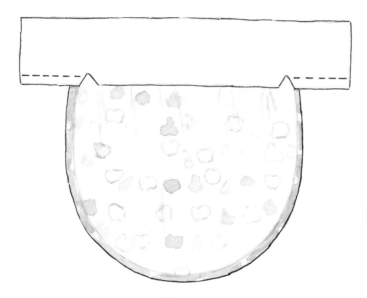

figure 2

10 Place the other waistband piece face down over the piece used in step 9, matching notches. Pin and sew the top and side edges, leaving the bottom notched edge unstitched. Clip the corners, and turn right side out.

11 Pin the apron front to the waistband, matching the notches, and baste. Turn the waistband inside out again. On the notched edge, stitch from each corner to the bias tape nearest it, making certain not to catch the tie ends in the seam (figure 2). Clip the corners.

12 Turn the waistband right side out and press. Topstitch the waistband closed ⅛ inch (3 mm) from the edge. Continue to topstitch around the entire waistband. Tie it on, and bake something sweet and gooey.

deep pockets

Materials

Apron kit (page 15)

Pattern (page 130)

⅝ yard (57.2 cm) of patterned fabric for the pocket

⅝ yard (57.2 cm) of solid fabric for the front

½ yard (45.7 cm) of fabric for the sash

38 inches (96.5 cm) of bias tape

What You Do

1 Cut one of each piece using the pattern pieces on page 130. Transfer the reverse of the fabric using tailor's chalk or a soft pencil.

2 Cut 5 inches (12.7 cm) of the bias tape, and fold it in half lengthwise. Press it. Stitch it to one corner of the front piece where marked on the pattern (figure 1). Repeat on the other corner.

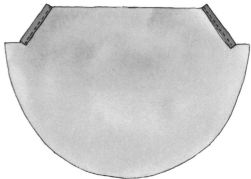

figure 1

3 Sew the bias tape to the upper curved edges of the pocket piece. To make this easier, first set a curve into the tape. Fold a 14-inch (35.6 cm) length in half lengthwise, and using an iron, curve it to the shape of the pocket, using the pattern as a guide. Pin it in place, and sew through all layers. Repeat for the second curve.

4 Lay the two pieces right sides together with the front piece on top. Stitch around the bottom curved edge, using a 5⁄8-inch (1.6 cm) seam allowance. Finish the raw edges if desired. Notch the curved seams to help it lie flat, but don't cut the notches too close to the stitching.

5 Turn the apron right side out, and press it down, making sure the curved seam is turned out fully. Pin the top center of the pocket carefully in place so that it matches the top of the front. Stitch down the middle of the apron to make two pockets.

6 Make the sash by cutting a rectangle 7 x 70 inches (17.8 x 177.8 cm). Fold the fabric in half lengthwise, right sides together. Cut each end at an angle. With a 1⁄2-inch (1.3 cm) seam allowance, sew up one short end and 27 inches (68.6 cm) along the long edge toward the middle. Repeat for the other end of the sash. You should have a 16-inch (40.6 cm) gap of raw edge. Turn the sash right side out, turning the raw edges under, and press it down.

7 Insert 1⁄2 inch (1.3 cm) of the apron front and pocket into the gap in the sash. Baste through all layers, making sure the bottom of the sash lines up neatly. Topstitch along the bottom edge of the sash, securing the apron body in place.

> *I enjoy using historical techniques and playing with shape, proportion, and structure. I let the nature of the fabric lead the design.*
>
> **—Ruth Singer**

the waldorf

Materials

Apron kit (page 15)

Pattern (page 120)

1¼ yards (1.1 m) of fabric (allow extra for matching patterns)

1 package (4 yards [3.7 m]) of ¼-inch-wide (6 mm) double-fold bias tape

Tools

Rotary cutter and mat (optional)

What You Do

1 Make the ties by cutting two rectangles, each 7 x 30 inches (17.8 x 76.2 cm). Fold each in half lengthwise, with the right sides together, to form two 3½ x 30-inch (8.9 x 76.2 cm) pieces. Press them both, and then, on each, sew the long sides together with a ½-inch (1.3 cm) seam.

2 On one open end, sew from the corner of the seamed side to the folded side at a 45° angle. Clip the corner, and trim the seams to ¼ inch (6 mm). Turn the tie right side out, and press it. Topstitch the three closed sides ⅛ inch (3 mm) from the edge. Repeat to finish the other tie, and set them both aside.

3 Following the pattern on page 120, cut the front piece on the fold.

4 Starting at a top edge of the fabric, pin the shorter fold of the bias tape to the front, right sides together. When you reach the scallops at the bottom, stretch the bias tape to fit around the curves, using as many pins as needed to keep the tape from shifting. Once you've pinned it all, stitch along the fold line, taking out the pins as you come to them. Take it slow and easy around the curves.

5 Fold the bias tape over the raw edge, and pin in place. Topstitch along the inside edge of the bias tape, catching it in back as you sew. Press.

6 Cut a rectangle 5 x 22 inches (12.7 x 55.9 cm) to make the waistband. Fold in each end ½ inch (1.3 cm), and press it down. Fold the waistband in half lengthwise, wrong sides together, and press it again. Open the waistband, and fold one raw edge ½ inch (1.3 cm) toward the wrong side, and press it in place.

7 To gather the apron front, sew ¼ inch (6 mm) from the raw edges and again at ⅜ inch (1 cm) from the raw edges using a long machine stitch. Pin the front piece to the front of the waistband, right sides together, matching centers and edges. Gather the fabric, distribute the gathers evenly, and pin them to the waistband. Sew a ½-inch (1.3 cm) seam, and then press the seam toward the waistband.

8 With the wrong side of the apron front facing up, flip the waistband down, covering the seam, and pin it in place. On the right side, topstitch the waistband ⅛ inch (3 mm) from the seam, catching back the waistband at the same time. Topstitch ⅛ inch (3 mm) from the edge, along the top edge of the waistband.

9 To attach the ties, hand pleat or gather the raw edge of the ties (page 16). Insert the tie ends into the waistband openings about ½ inch (1.3 cm), making sure that the longer side edge of the tie is aligned with the top of the waistband. Stitch the ties in place ⅛ inch (3 mm) from the waistband edge.

josephine

Materials

Apron kit (page 15)

Pattern (page 129)

1 yard (91.4 cm) each of two fabrics—A and B—for the reversible bodice and front bottom

1 yard (90 cm) of a complementary fabric for the neck strap, waistband, ties, and drawstrings

1 yard (90 cm) of muslin

Tear-away stabilizer

Tools

Rotary mat, clear ruler with 45° angle lines, and cutter

Seam ripper

What You Do

1 Enlarge the front bottom template on page 129, and cut it out. Place fabric A, unfolded, on the work surface. Refer to figure 1 (next page) to get all the pieces out of 1 yard (90 cm) of material. Pin the front bottom to the fabric, and mark the bodice, casing, and bias strips for the ruffle. Cut out all the pieces. Place fabric B, unfolded, on the work surface and repeat.

2 Place the complementary fabric, folded widthwise, on the work surface and, using the schematic in figure 2 (next page), cut out the drawstrings, neck straps, and ties. Cut out the single waistband last, unfolding the fabric to get enough material.

3 To make the neck strap, press ½ inch (1.3 cm) under on each long edge. Fold the strap in half lengthwise and press. Topstitch along each edge.

4 To make the drawstrings, fold each in half lengthwise and press. Open the fold, and press each edge in toward the center. Fold again along the original pressed fold, and topstitch along each edge.

5 Make buttonholes in the bodice casing through which to thread the drawstrings. Mark the center point of one casing piece. Using this as a reference, move ¾ inch (1.9 cm) down into the fabric to mark the spot to make a ½-inch (1.3 cm) buttonhole. Use the tear-away stabilizer to reinforce the hole as you construct it, following the instructions for your sewing machine. Slice the buttonhole open with the seam ripper. Repeat for the second casing piece.

6 Pin and stitch one bodice casing piece made from fabric A to one bodice piece made of fabric B, with right sides together. Stitch the other casing made out of fabric B to the bodice in fabric A. Trim the seams, and press them toward the bodice.

" The minute I saw the fabric I ended up using for the sashes, the idea of a reversible apron popped into my mind. "
—Valerie Shrader

61

7 Baste one end of one drawstring to the wrong side of either casing (figure 3). Don't push it through the buttonhole yet. Baste the other drawstring to the other side. Baste the strap to the same bodice, placing it ⅝ inch (1.6 cm) from the side, with the raw edges even with the raw edges of the casing (figure 4). Be careful not to twist the strap.

8 Pin both bodice pieces together, with right sides together, aligning the seams and matching the center points. Beginning and ending ½ inch (1.3 cm) from the bottom edge, stitch along the sides and top, leaving the entire bottom open, being careful not to catch the drawstrings or straps in the stitching (figure 5, page 64). Trim the seam of the casing only, at the buttonholes, to ⅛ inch (3 mm) to allow the drawstrings to come from either side. Reinforce the stitching at the upper corners of the casing. Turn it right side out.

9 To create the channel for the drawstrings within the casing, pin across the top of the casing, and topstitch close to the edge. Thread the strings through one buttonhole to the right side, and pin in place in the center of the channel. Using a zipper foot if necessary, topstitch along the bottom of the casing as close to the existing seam as possible.

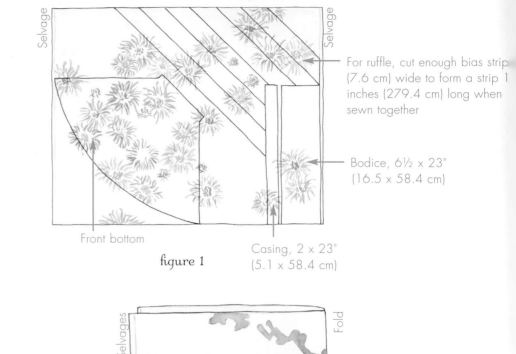

For ruffle, cut enough bias strip (7.6 cm) wide to form a strip 1 inches (279.4 cm) long when sewn together

Bodice, 6½ x 23" (16.5 x 58.4 cm)

Selvage

Selvage

Front bottom

Casing, 2 x 23" (5.1 x 58.4 cm)

figure 1

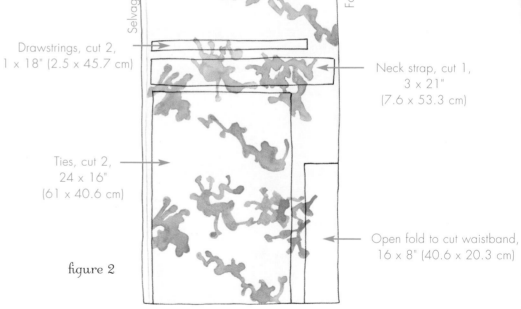

Selvages

Fold

Drawstrings, cut 2, 1 x 18" (2.5 x 45.7 cm)

Neck strap, cut 1, 3 x 21" (7.6 x 53.3 cm)

Ties, cut 2, 24 x 16" (61 x 40.6 cm)

Open fold to cut waistband, 16 x 8" (40.6 x 20.3 cm)

figure 2

10 Knot the ends of the drawstrings. (When you reverse the apron, untie the knots and slip the strings through the buttonhole on the other "right" side of the casing. Knot them again to secure.)

11 Mark the center points of the bottom edge of the bodice pieces. Gather the bottom edge of the bodice pieces, using long basting stitches.

figure 3

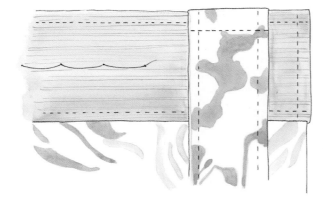

figure 4

12 Make the ties and waistband. For the ties, first cut the two 24 x 16-inch (61 x 40.6 cm) tie pieces in half lengthwise to yield four 24 x 8-inch (61 x 20.3 cm) pieces. Stack and cut them again to yield eight 24 x 4-inch (61 x 10.2 cm) pieces. For the waistband, cut the 16 x 8-inch (40.6 x 20.3 cm) waistband piece in half lengthwise to yield two 16 x 4-inch (40.6 x 10.2 cm) pieces. Mark the center point of each waistband piece. Construct the first waistband/tie with four tie pieces and one waistband piece. Stitch the two tie pieces together along the short edges, right sides facing. Repeat for the other two pieces. Sew the waistband between these pieces, right sides together, leaving the side seam open ½ inch (1.3 cm) on either side of the bottom of the waistband (the edge that you'll sew to the front bottom). See figure 6, page 64. Repeat to make the second waistband/tie, but stitch all the seams completely.

13 Stitch the first waistband/tie piece—the one with the open seam—to the bodice, with the right side together with the fabric A side, along the top of the waistband section only, gathering the bodice to fit and matching side seams and center points. Begin and end the stitching at the ½-inch (1.3 cm) seam left open in step 8 (figure 7). Repeat for the reverse side of the waistband/tie and the bodice.

14 With the bodice inside out and the right sides of the waistband/tie together, stitch the long edges and short ends of the ties together, stitching to the ½-inch (1.3 cm) side seam left open on the waistband in step 12 and leaving the front section free. Trim the seams, and turn the waistband/tie right side out. Press it down.

15 Construct a ruffle by cutting strips from fabric A on the bias (figure 1, on page 62) and piecing them to get one strip 110 inches (2.8 m) long. Repeat to construct a second ruffle from fabric B. With the right sides facing, stitch the ruffle pieces together, leaving one long edge open. Trim the seam, turn it right side out, and press it down. Mark the center point of the ruffle.

16 Gather the raw edges of the ruffle using two rows of basting stitches. Pin them to the bottom of one front bottom piece, beginning and ending ½ inch (1.3 cm) from the side edge. Connect the fabric A side of the ruffle to the front bottom of fabric B. With the marks aligned and the raw edges even, baste the ruffle to the front bottom piece. Trim the seam.

17 With the right sides facing, pin and stitch both front bottom pieces together along the sides and hem, leaving the waist open. Begin and

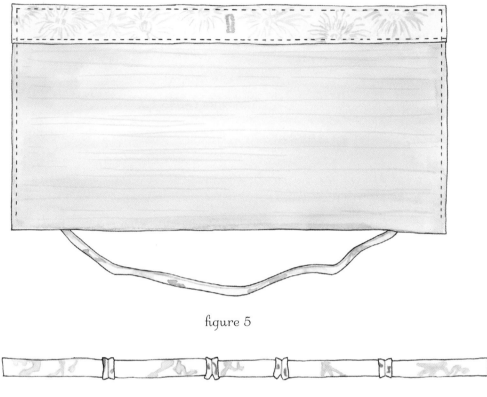

figure 5

figure 6

end the seam ½ inch (1.3 cm) below the waistline.

18 Pin the fabric A front bottom piece to the same side of the fabric A bodice, right sides facing. Stitch them together.

19 Turn and press under the seam allowance on the remaining waistband/tie. Place it on the ½-inch (1.3 cm) seamline of the fabric B front bottom piece, and slipstitch the opening closed. Decide which pretty side you

feel like showing off today, cinch it on, and give a little sashay because you look so good!

figure 7

Designer Joan Hand Stroh

Lorelei

Materials

Apron kit (page 15)

Pattern (page 135)

⅞ yard (80 cm) of floral fabric

¼ yard (22.9 cm) of checked fabric

6¼ yards (5.7 m) of ¼-inch (6 mm) double-fold bias tape

1 yard (91.4 cm) of ½-inch (1.3 cm) rickrack

Tool

Seam leveler

What You Do

1 Cut out the apron pieces following the pattern on page 135. Transfer the dots from the front pattern piece onto the fabric. Next, trim the outer edges to accept bias tape. Without pulling or stretching the edges, set the pieces aside. If necessary, splice the bias tape together.

2 With right sides together, stitch two pocket pieces together along the top, using a ¼ inch (6 mm) seam allowance and inserting rickrack between them (page 19). Flip them right side out and press. Bind the outside edges of the pocket, folding under the ends of the bias tape at the top side of each pocket. Repeat to create the second pocket.

3 At the pattern's pocket corner dots, pin the pockets to the front of the apron. Stitch around the outside edge of the pocket, reinforcing the stitch at each top edge.

4 Attach bias tape along the inner curved edge of the neck strap. With wrong sides together, pin the neck strap to the top front so that the notches align (figure 1).

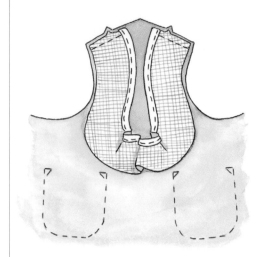

figure 1

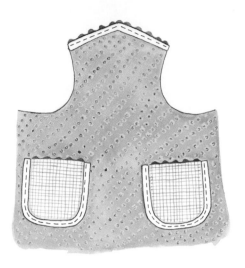

figure 2

5 Insert rickrack under the top front before sewing on the outer edge of the bias tape (figure 2). Bind the outside edges of the apron front and the neck strap.

6 To create the tie, fold under the long side twice to make a ⅜-inch (1 cm) double hem. Press and stitch. To make a point, fold one end of the tie diagonally with right sides together, and then stitch it down along the long side, ⅜ inch (1 cm) from the edge. Turn the corner right side out, press, and then stitch the remaining long edge of the tie with a ⅜-inch (1 cm) double hem. Topstitch the point. Finally, create a

pleat in the raw end of the tie that attaches to the apron (page 16). Repeat for the other tie, and then pin each tie to the apron with wrong sides together.

7 Bind the remaining outer edges of the apron, folding under the edges and stitching close to the edge of the bias tape. For added strength, reinforce the stitching where the ties connect to the apron. Put it on, call for take-out, and kick up your heels.

> "For months after cutting and tweaking this pattern, I struggled with which fabrics to use. One day, I glanced at some cloth—there it was, almost as if the fabrics had waved and shouted. Fabric really will speak to you."
> —Joan Hand Stroh

little master

Materials

Apron kit (page 15)

Pattern (page 119)

¼ yard (22.9 cm) of blue fabric

1 yard (91.4 cm) of red fabric

8½ x 11-inch (21.6 x 27.9 cm) piece of cardboard

2 green buttons, each 1 inch (2.5 cm) in diameter

1½-inch (3.8 cm) bit of hook-and-loop tape (both sides)

What You Do

1 Cut two circles from the cardboard, one 8½ inches (21.6 cm) in diameter and the other 3 inches (7.6 cm) in diameter. Lay the large cardboard pattern on the blue fabric, and cut out two circles, each ¼ inch (6 mm) larger than the pattern all the way around. Cut out one smaller circle the same way. Use these pieces to make three yo-yos (page 20).

2 Sew the green buttons over the openings in the two large yo-yos.

3 Using the pattern (page 119), cut out the apron pieces. Mark the pocket placement on the front piece. Mark notches for the belt placement. For the belt, cut two rectangles out of the red fabric, each 5 x 4 inches (12.7 x 10.2 cm).

4 To make the bias strips for binding the armhole openings, cut two strips from the red fabric, each 1½ x 13 inches (3.8 x 33 cm). Stitching as many pieces as necessary, stitch together another strip 1½ x 64 inches (3.8 x 162.6 cm) to use for binding the back and neckline. Turn in one long edge of each bias strip ½ inch (1.3 cm), and press it down. This will help you turn a clean edge after sewing the strips in place.

" I like really vibrant colors and I always go for high contrast. The rules say to choose complementary colors, but I'm almost always happier selecting shades on either side of the complement. "

—Wendi Gratz

5 Stitch the pockets into place on the front, leaving the top 3½ inches (8.9 cm) of each yo-yo unstitched for the pocket opening.

6 Fold one belt piece in half, right sides together, to create a 4 x 2½-inch (10.2 x 6.4 cm) rectangle. Sew down the open long edge and one short side. Snip off the excess seam allowance at the corner, turn it right side out, and press it down. Repeat with the other belt piece.

7 Join the front piece to the back at the shoulders and sides using a ⅝-inch (1.6 cm) seam allowance. Press all the seams open.

8 Pin the belt rectangles on the right side of the back pieces where marked on the pattern, matching the raw edges (figure 1).

9 Attach the bias strip to the back and neckline. Start at the bottom of the back opening. Lay the bias strip with right side facing the right side of the fabric, raw edges together, and stitch all the way up one side of the back, around the neckline, and down the other side of the back, catching the belt at the waist. Trim away the seam allowance to about ¼ inch (6 mm), and clip around the curves.

figure 1

10 Fold the bias strip to the back along the stitched line, and press it down. You should have a nice seam at the garment opening and a clean fold on the inside, ready to be stitched down. Stitch down the folded edge of the bias strip close to the fold. It will show as topstitching on the right side of the apron.

11 Using the same method outlined in steps 9 and 10, attach the bias strips around the armholes.

12 To make the bottom hem of the apron, turn the bottom edge up ½ inch (1.3 cm), and press it down. Turn it up another ½ inch (1.3 cm), press, and stitch it down.

13 Stitch both halves of the hook-and-loop tape into place on the two belt pieces (figure 2).

14 Hand sew the small yo-yo over the hook-and-loop tape, stitching on the overlapping belt piece. Now sit back and wait for the next masterpiece for your fridge.

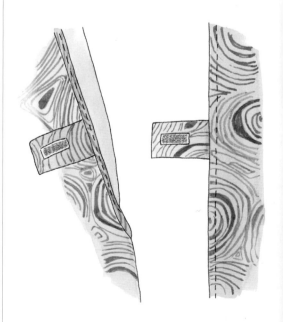

figure 2

mango tango

Materials

Apron kit (page 15)

Pattern (page 134)

1 yard (91.4 cm) of floral fabric

9 yards (8.2 m) of ¼-inch (6 mm) double-fold bias tape

Tool

Seam leveler

What You Do

1 Make a true bias fold of the fabric, as shown in figure 1 (next page). Next, cut the apron pieces, using the pattern on page 134. Transfer the dots on the bottom front pattern onto the fabric. Without pulling or stretching the edges of the pattern pieces, trim all the outer edges to accept the bias tape, and set the pieces aside.

2 Stitch the neck strap pieces together at the center back, right sides together. Press. Attach bias tape to the inner edge of the neck strap.

3 Fold a strip of bias tape in half lengthwise. Pin it to the top front, 2 inches (5.1 cm) away from the upper edge and parallel to it. Topstitch.

4 Baste the neck strap to the top front, with the wrong sides together.

5 Bind the top edge of the top front (figure 2), including the bottom edges of the neck strap. Press the top front and the neck strap flat.

6 With right sides together and the centers of the pattern pieces aligned, stitch the bottom edge of the top front and tie to the top edge of the bottom front (figure 3).

> **"** A good apron becomes like a second skin; you forget you've got it on. If you look flirty in it, well, so much the better! **"**
>
> —**Joan Hand Stroh**

73

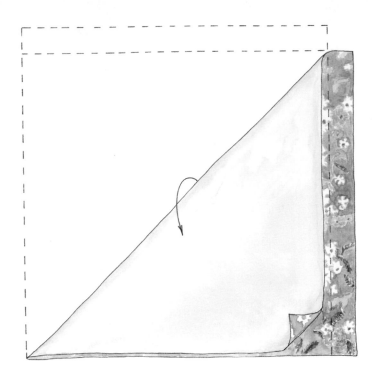

figure 1

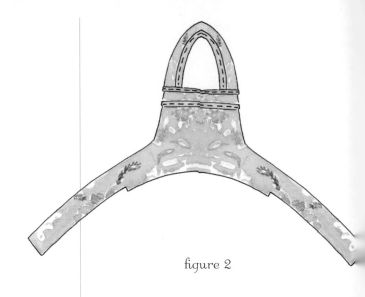

figure 2

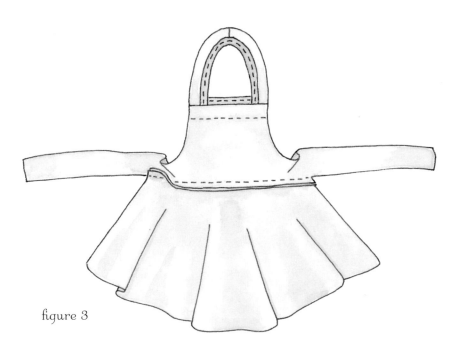

figure 3

7 Trim and bind the edges of the seam. Attach bias tape along the remaining edges of the apron, mitering the corners as needed.

8 Bind the open edge of the pocket, trimming the bias even with the outside edges. Then bind the outer edges of the pocket using a basting stitch and bias tape, mitering the corners.

9 Position the pocket on top of the skirt, matching the corners to the dots on the pattern, and pin it there securely. Fold the pocket edges under approximately ⅜ inch (1 cm). Stitch the pocket in place using a seam leveler at the beginning, end, and corners if necessary. After putting it on, you'll be ready to dance across the kitchen in your new favorite apron.

provence smock

Materials

Apron kit (page 15)

Pattern (page 132)

1½ yards (1.4 m) of toile

¼ yard (22.9 cm) of white cotton to line pockets

8 yards (7.3 m) of ¼-inch (6 mm) double-fold bias tape

Fusible interfacing, 4-inch (10.2 cm) square

2 each, ¾-inch (1.9 cm) vintage mother-of-pearl buttons

Tool

Seam leveler

What You Do

1 Cut out the apron pieces using the pattern on page 132. Trim all the outer edges of the fabric pieces to accept the bias tape. Set them aside.

2 If necessary, splice the bias tape together to create one long piece. Save the spliced bias for binding the outer edges of the apron, where the splice will be easier to hide.

3 Attach the bias tape; to do so, start stitching 1 inch (2.5 cm) ahead of where the bias meets the fabric, so the stitches are even and clean. Stitch close to the inner edge, attaching the bias tape across the top front of the apron.

4 Cut two strips of fusible interfacing 1 x 4 inches (2.5 x 10.2 cm), and press them on the wrong side of the neck straps where the two button-holes will be.

5 Trim *one* of the yoke pieces ⅜ inch (1 cm) away from the lower edge between the circles. This piece will become the yoke front; the remaining one will be the lining. Do not trim the lining.

Everyone loves the crisscross back. Women who buy it tell me they'll wear it as a fashion statement or to dress up T-shirts.

—Joan Hand Stroh

6 Sew the pocket front and the lining together using a ⅜-inch (1 cm) seam. Press it down. Trim all but ¼ inch (6 mm) away from the seam. Turn, and press it down. Run two gathering lines across the top of the pocket, and set it aside.

7 Run two gathering lines across the top of the apron front. Set it aside.

8 Join the neck straps to the yoke and yoke lining. Press the seams open.

9 Sandwich the yoke and yoke lining together. Baste or stitch them with the longest machine stitch through the center and around the inside edges of the neck strap. Press it down, making sure all the edges are evenly aligned. Trim them if necessary.

10 Mark the buttonholes on the right side of the neck straps, and then make the holes.

11 Attach the apron front to the yoke lining, with the right side of the lining to the wrong side of the front. Match the notches and the center front. Adjust the gathers, and stitch them together with a ⅝-inch (1.6 cm) seam (figure 1). Press the seam to the yoke.

Remove the gathering threads, and trim the seam to ½ inch (1.3 cm), clipping the curves if necessary.

12 Baste or closely pin the yoke over the gathered edge of the apron front.

13 Encase the right-side edge of the yoke with the bias tape (figure 2). Allow for ½ inch (1.3 cm) on each side of the dots. Stitch through all the thicknesses.

14 Encase the outer edges of the apron front. Begin at the inside edge of the left neck strap. Bind the inner neck strap, continuing around the yoke. Miter the right corner of the neck strap, and continue along the outer edge, covering the exposed edge of the bias tape on the front of the yoke. When you reach the outside edge of the left strap, finish off by turning in the edge and stitching through all thicknesses.

15 Pull the gathers on the pocket to equal 5 inches (12.7 cm) across. Bind the top edge with the bias tape, leaving ½ inch (1.3 cm) on each side. Remove the gathering stitches. Position the pocket on the apron front. Turn the bias edges under, and stitch close to the edge all around the pocket. Use the seam leveler at the corners as necessary.

16 Make the ties for each pocket by cutting two pieces of bias tape, each 15 inches (38.1 cm) long. Press them open, fold them over, and stitch them with a ¼-inch (6 mm) seam. Turn and press them. Turn under each end, and hand stitch them closed. Tie them into bows, and stitch them to the desired location on each pocket. (Alternatively, topstitch the outside of the bias tape, and tie each end tightly into a knot.)

17 Cut two small squares or dots of interfacing, and fuse them to the wrong side of the neck straps where you will sew the buttons. Sew the buttons through the fabric and interfacing.

figure 1

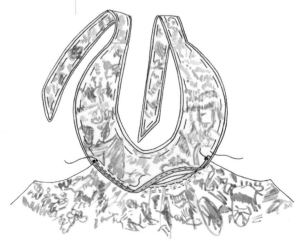

figure 2

Designer **Erin Harris**

orange crush

Materials

Apron kit (page 15)

Small amounts of 10 printed fabrics for the patchwork and the towel loop

¾ yard (68.6 cm) of natural-colored linen or cotton for the front

¾ yard (68.6 cm) of muslin for the lining

¼ yard (22.9 cm) of floral print for the pocket

¾ yard (68.6 cm) of gingham for the waistband and ties

6 inches (15.2 cm) of lace for the pocket

¾ yard (68.6 cm) each of three different laces, in varying widths but at least ½ inch (1.3 cm) wide for the patchwork

Tools

Rotary cutter and mat (optional)

Seam allowance:
¼ inch (6 mm)
unless otherwise noted

What You Do

1 Cut all the pieces you'll need using the schematic (figure 1, page 82) as your guide. You'll cut the lace later as described in subsequent steps.

2 To make the pocket, use the 6-inch (15.2 cm) piece of lace. Lay the larger pocket-lining piece right side up. Lay the lace on top of it, wrong side up, and then the smaller pocket front, also wrong side up, matching the top edges. Pin and then sew them all together. Press the seam toward the larger pocket piece.

3 Match the bottom edge of the pocket front end to end with the pocket lining, right sides together. Press it flat. Turn both bottom edges ¼ inch (6 mm) toward the wrong side, and press it again. Pin the pocket together along the sides, and then sew up the sides. Turn it right side out, and press it again.

4 Pin the pocket to the apron front 4½ inches (11.4 cm) from the side edge and 6 inches (15.2 cm) from the top edge. Sew it in place by topstitching ⅛ inch (3 mm) along the pocket sides and bottom.

5 To make the towel loop, fold the 4 x 7-inch (10.2 x 17.8 cm) rec-

> *Patchwork strips and delicate lace give this apron a vintage, old-fashioned charm, while the graphic prints and simple lines look contemporary.*
> **—Erin Harris**

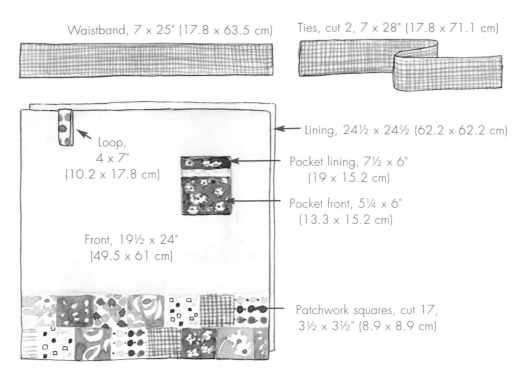

Waistband, 7 x 25" (17.8 x 63.5 cm)

Ties, cut 2, 7 x 28" (17.8 x 71.1 cm)

Lining, 24½ x 24½ (62.2 x 62.2 cm)

Loop,
4 x 7"
(10.2 x 17.8 cm)

Pocket lining, 7½ x 6"
(19 x 15.2 cm)

Pocket front, 5¼ x 6"
(13.3 x 15.2 cm)

Front, 19½ x 24"
(49.5 x 61 cm)

Patchwork squares, cut 17,
3½ x 3½" (8.9 x 8.9 cm)

figure 1

tangle in half lengthwise, wrong sides together, and press. Open it, bring in the side edges toward the middle fold, and press again. Fold it in half again, and press once more. Pin it together along its open side, and topstitch ⅛ inch (3 mm) from each side edge. Line up both raw edges with the top edge of the apron, 3 inches (7.6 cm) in from the side. Sew it in place ¼ inch (6 mm) from the top edge.

6 Assemble the patchwork squares into two strips: one eight squares long and one nine squares long. Sew them together, and press the seams open.

7 Pin a length of the lace to the top edge of the longer patchwork piece, right side up, and baste it in place ⅛ inch (3 mm) from the edge. Trim away any extra lace. Pin the patchwork strips right sides together, centering the shorter piece like brickwork above the longer piece so the seams don't line up (figure 2). Sew the strips together. Press the seam toward the shorter strip and the lace toward the longer strip. Trim the edges of the longer patchwork strip, so it's even with the shorter one (figure 3).

8 Pin the second length of lace to the top edge of the patchwork, right side up, and baste it in place ⅛ inch (3 mm) from the edge. Trim away any extra lace. Pin the patchwork strip to the apron front, right sides together, and sew it using a ¼-inch (6 mm) seam. Press the seam toward the apron front and the lace toward the patchwork.

9 Cut a piece of lace 24½ inches (62.2 cm) long. Hem the edges by turning ⅛ inch (3 mm) toward the wrong side, and then turning ⅛ inch (3 mm) again, and stitching in place.

Pin it to the bottom edge of the patchwork, right sides together, lining up raw edges, starting and ending ¼ inch (6 mm) in from the ends. Baste it in place ⅛ inch (3 mm) from the edge.

10 To make the ties, fold each rectangle in half lengthwise with right sides together to form two 3½ x 28-inch (8.9 x 71.1 cm) pieces. Press them, and then sew each long side with a ½-inch (1.3 cm) seam. On one open end, sew a ½-inch (1.3 cm) seam. Clip the corners, and trim the seams to ¼ inch (6 mm). Turn each tie right side out, and press it again. Topstitch the three closed sides of each tie ⅛ inch (3 mm) from the edge.

11 Pin the apron front to the lining, right sides together, and sew ¼-inch (6 mm) seams along the sides and the bottom, being careful not to catch the lace in the side seams. Turn it right side out and press. Sew the lining to the front ¼ inch (6 mm) from the top edge.

12 Fold each end of the waistband in ½ inch (1.3 cm) and press. Then fold the waistband in half lengthwise, wrong sides together, and press. Open the waistband, and fold one raw edge ½ inch (1.3 cm) toward the wrong side, and press it in place.

13 Pin the apron front to the front of the waistband, right sides together, matching the edges. Sew a

½-inch (1.3 cm) seam. Press the seam toward the waistband. With the wrong side of the apron facing up, flip the waistband down, covering the seam, and pin it in place. On the right side, stitch the waistband ⅛ inch (3 mm) from the seam, catching the back of the waistband at the same time. Topstitch ⅛ inch (3 mm) from the edge along the top of the waistband.

14 To attach the ties, insert the raw edge of each tie about ½ inch (1.3 cm) into the waistband opening on each side. Stitch in place ⅛ inch (3 mm) from the waistband edge.

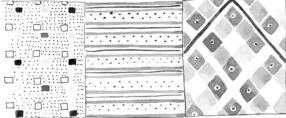

figure 2

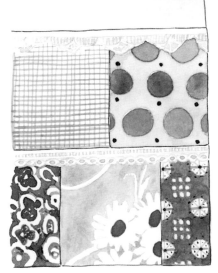
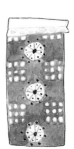

figure 3

marie antoinette

Materials

Apron kit (page 15)

Pattern (page 130)

½ yard (45.7 cm) of muslin

½ yard (45.7 cm) of embroidered silk taffeta, 54 inches
(1.4 m) wide

⅛ yard (11.4 cm) of silk dupioni, 45 inches (1.1 m) wide

½ yard (45.7 cm) of embellished polyester organza,
60 inches (1.5 m) wide

2 yards (1.8 m) of tulle,
54 inches (1.4 m) wide

¼ yard (22.9 cm) of silk chiffon,
45 inches (1.1 m) wide

Vintage sequins

Embroidery floss

Tools

Rotary cutter, cutting mat,
and ruler

What You Do

1 Enlarge the underskirt template on page 130, and use it to cut the pattern out of the muslin. Mark the center point of the waist and hem. Cut out the other pieces according to the chart in figure 1 (next page). Cut the front and ties out of the silk organza; the waistband and yo-yos out of the silk dupioni; the bottom ruffle out of the polyester organza; the center ruffle out of the tulle; and the top ruffle out of the silk chiffon. Mark the center point of the waist and hem of the front piece.

2 Make ½-inch (1.3 cm) narrow hems along the 17-inch (43.2 cm) sides of the underskirt. Do the same for the bottom edge, mitering the corners (page 21).

3 Make a ½-inch (1.3 cm) narrow hem at the lower edge and each 18-inch (45.7 cm) edge of the front. Stitch a row of basting stitches across the waistline.

4 To make the bottom ruffle, fold the polyester organza in half lengthwise, and baste it together along the long raw edges (figure 2). Mark the center point.

5 Draw a line 1 inch (2.5 cm) above the bottom of the underskirt, and then mark its center point. Gather

"After I found the silk taffeta, nothing else would do! It's actually meant for home decorating, but it was perfect for this fancy, 'frothy' apron."

—Valerie Shrader

the bottom ruffle evenly to fit the underskirt along that line. Matching the center points, pin the gathered ruffle to the right side of the underskirt along the line. Stitch it in place.

6 To make the center ruffle, repeat steps 4 and 5 with the tulle, except draw the line on the underskirt 2 inches (5.1 cm) above the bottom ruffle.

7 To make the top ruffle, repeat steps 4 and 5 with the silk chiffon, placing the line 1 inch (2.5 cm) above the center ruffle.

8 Stitch two ties together along the short ends, right sides facing. Stitch two more together in the same fashion. Sew one waistband piece between these two sections, right sides facing, leaving the side seam open ½ inch (1.3 cm) on either side of the bottom of the waistband-the edge you will sew to the apron front. See figure 3.

9 Repeat step 8 with the remaining ties and waistband, stitching all the seams completely this time. This is the waistband lining. Stitch it to the waistband front, right sides together, leaving the bottom open. Trim the seam, turn it over, and press it down.

10 Baste the underskirt to the apron front, matching center points and gathering the front to fit.

Ties, cut 8,
3½ x 17"
(8.9 x 43.2 cm)

Yo-yos, cut 3, 4
(10.2 cm) in
diameter

Waistband, cut 2,
3½ x 17" (8.9 x 43.2 cm)

Front, 18 x 27"
(45.7 x 68.6 cm)

Top ruffle,
9 x 45"
(22.9 x 114.3 cm)

Center ruffle,
10 x 72"
(25.4 x 182.9 cm)

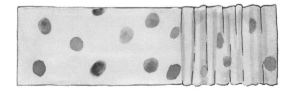

Bottom ruffle,
10 x 60"
(25.4 x 152.4 cm)

figure 1

11 Stitch the front of the waistband—the edge with the open ½-inch (1.3 cm) section of seam—to the apron front, right sides together. Fold the waistband up, and press the waistband lining under on the seam line. Stitch the lining to the underskirt by hand.

12 Along one side of the apron, slipstitch the edges of the front and the underskirt together. On the other side, make an accordion-folded pleat to gather the fabric close to the top of the top ruffle. Tack it in place (figure 4). Make a narrow fold at the side of the ruffle below the tack, and slipstitch it to the underskirt. Continue stitching to sew the edge of the front to the edge of the underskirt.

13 Make another accordion pleat about two-thirds of the way across the hem of the front. Tack it together. Fold one side edge of the bottom ruffle diagonally up to the underskirt, and tack it to the hem (figure 5). Repeat on the other edge.

14 To make the decorative yo-yos, refer to page 20. Stitch one yo-yo to the waist. Tack the others in place over the accordion pleats. Add additional embellishments, such as sequins held on with colorful embroidery floss. Tie on your new apron, find a party, and float around looking divine.

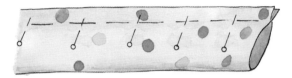

figure 2

figure 3

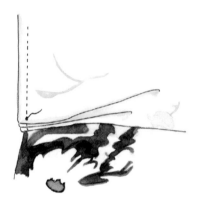

figure 4

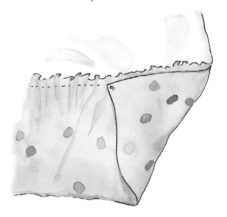

figure 5

pop beads

Materials

Apron kit (page 15)

Pattern (page 125)

1½ yards (1.4 m)
of patterned fabric

16 inches (40.6 cm) of ¾-inch
(1.9 cm) grosgrain ribbon

4¼ yards (3.9 m)
of pleated trim with lip

Seam allowance:

¼ inch (6 mm)

unless otherwise noted

What You Do

1 Use the pattern (page 125) to cut out the apron pieces.

2 Attach the grosgrain ribbon to the top and curved edges of the pocket.

3 Pin each pocket, right sides up, to the front side piece, aligned with the pattern's pocket line and the dot (figure 1). Stitch as close to the edge as possible around the curved side of the pocket, and baste the inside raw edges.

4 Baste the apron front to the front side with wrong sides together.

5 Apply the pleated trim over the front seams. Press the seams toward the sides. Attach the grosgrain ribbon over the outside edge of the pleated trim.

6 In both back pattern pieces, make a dart and then press toward the center. With the right sides together, stitch the front sides to the back pieces.

7 Attach the pleated trim to the right side of the apron's outer edges. Next, apply the grosgrain ribbon over the pleated trim.

figure 1

8 Pin and stitch the top of the apron front to the waistband between the small dots and with right sides together. Trim the seam, and then press the seam and the waistband out. Fold and press the solid edge of the waistband under ½ inch (1.3 cm), and then trim to ¼ inch (6 mm).

9 To make each tie, fold under ⅜ inch (1 cm) on the long sides and the end without the dots. Press under the raw edges, and miter the corners (page 21) on the end without the dots. Squaring the stitches at the mitered corners, stitch the hem. Fold the end of the tie diagonally over the wrong side, and stitch it in place along the long side. Create a pleat (page 16) in the remaining end of the tie and baste. Repeat to create the other tie.

10 Pin and then baste the pleated tie ends to the waistband between the dots, with right sides together. Fold the waistband along the center lengthwise, with right sides together, and stitch both ends to secure the ties. Trim the corners and the seams.

11 Turn the waistband right side out and press. Covering the waist seam, pin down and then topstitch the free long edge of the waistband.

psychedelic squares

Materials

Apron kit (page 15)

Pattern (page 131)

1 yard (91.4 cm)
of fabric for the front

½ yard (45.7 cm)
of complementary fabric

Double-fold bias tape

Marking chalk

What You Do

1 Enlarge and cut out the pattern pieces (page 131). Press a crease down the center of the front piece to use in placing the pocket later. Cut a strip of double-fold bias tape a little longer than the top of the pocket.

2 Press the pocket and the pocket binding. Place the top of the pocket between the binding, and pin it.

3 Stitch the binding to the pocket using the left side of the presser foot as a guide. Be sure the binding is sewn on the wrong side as well. Then press the pocket, and snip the excess binding and threads.

4 To make the ties, fold each in half lengthwise, with right sides together and raw edges matching. Press.

5 Stitch the ties with a ¼-inch (6 mm) seam allowance. Pivot ¼ inch (6 mm) from the end, and stitch the end of the tie. Snip the corner of the sewn tie.

6 Turn the tie inside out using a rod or chopstick, and push out the corners. Press the ties flat and even.

7 Finish the ties by topstitching ¼ inch (6 mm) from the sewn edge on two sides.

8 To make the front apron piece, start with its sides. Fold in ¼ to ½ inch (6 mm to 1.3 cm) along the edges and press. Fold again to create a double fold, and press again. Pin the folded sides after pressing.

9 Stitch both sides using the left side of your presser foot as a guide. Press again.

10 Determine the top and bottom of the apron then repeat steps 8 and 9 for those edges: with the fabric right side up, double fold, pin, stitch, and press.

11 Turn the fabric right side down, and fold in the sides and bottom ½ inch (1.3 cm). Press.

" I like the fabrics to speak for themselves, so I don't embellish heavily. "
—Carrie Sommer

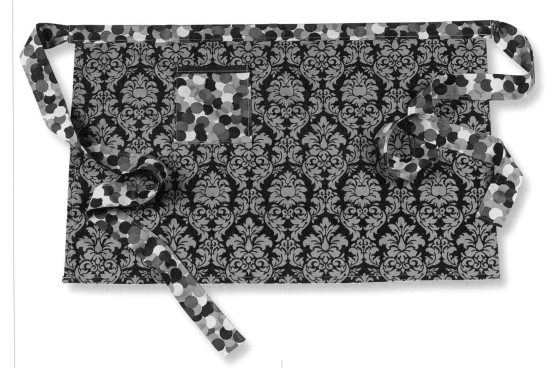

12 Using the center fold as a guide, place the pocket 2 inches (5.1 cm) to the right of the fold and 4½ inches (11.4 cm) down from the top. Pin it in place, and then stitch close to the edge, using the right side of the presser foot as a guide.

13 To make the waistband, turn the cut piece of fabric over so the wrong side is facing up, and fold the ends in 1 inch (2.5 cm). Press the folds.

14 Fold in the cut edge of the fabric ¼ inch (6 mm), and press it. Fold the wrong sides of the fabric together, and press it again.

15 Open, and place the apron front (right side up) flush against the center folded seam (figure 1). Press in place, and pin the two pieces together.

16 Stitch on the waistband using the left side of the presser foot as a guide.

17 To attach the ties, lay the apron out, right side up. Position the ties so the topstitching on each tie lines up with the topstitching of the waistband. Create a pleat with your finger to make the ties the same size as the waistband, and then insert the ties into the folded end of the waistband (figure 2).

18 Stitch along the opening three or four times to create a strong seam. Plan a party: You're going to want to show this one off.

figure 1

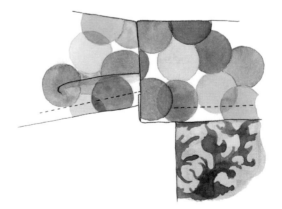

figure 2

Designer Nathalie Mornu

Spotless

Materials

Apron kit (see page 15)

¾ yard (68.6 cm)
of printed fabric for the front

18 x 22-inch (45.7 x 55.9 cm)
piece of printed fabric
for the front panel

¼ yard (22.9 cm)
of printed fabric for the pockets

1 yard (91.4 cm) of ribbon

2 yards (1.8 m) of 1-inch
(2.5 cm) shirring tape
(sold in the drapery department
of fabric stores)

2 large buttons

What You Do

1 Referring to the schematic (figure 1), cut out all the fabric pieces.

2 Make a ½-inch (1.3 cm) hem on the long sides and at the bottom of the front, mitering the corners (page 21). Also make a ½-inch (1.3 cm) hem on the long sides and bottom of the panel, again mitering the corners.

3 Place the panel face up on the work surface, and pin the ribbon along the right-hand edge, turning it under at the top and bottom to hide the cut. Topstitch along both edges of the ribbon.

4 Hem the top edges of each pocket by turning under one of the short sides ¼ inch (6 mm), press, then turn it under ¾ inch (1.9 cm). Press and top-stitch. Turn under the remaining sides ½ inch (1.3 cm) and press then miter the corners (page 21).

5 With the panel right side up on your work surface, pin one pocket, right side up, 4 inches (10.2 cm) below the top edge and 5½ inches (14 cm) from the edge trimmed with ribbon. Pin the remaining pocket 2½ inches (6.4 cm) below the bottom of the first. Topstitch both pockets ⅛ inch (3 mm) from the side and bottom edges, leaving the tops open.

"Embellishing is my favorite part. The moment I select the main fabric, I dash over to the trims to see what will work with it."
—Nathalie Mornu

6 Place the apron front right side up on your work surface. Pin the panel to it, right side up, matching the top and left edges. Baste along the top edge.

7 To make the casing, fold the basted edge under ¼ inch (6 mm) and press. Fold under 1¼ inch (3.2 cm). Press, pin, and then topstitch it close to the fold.

8 Attach a safety pin to one end of the shirring tape, and run the tape through the casing. Center the apron on the tape, and use pins to mark the spots where both sides of the tape exit from the casing. Slide the apron along the casing toward the middle to reveal some of the hidden tape. Mark a spot from each pin, 2½ inches (6.4 cm) toward the center, and sew a button at each spot (figure 2). Trim the shirring tape if the ties are too long.

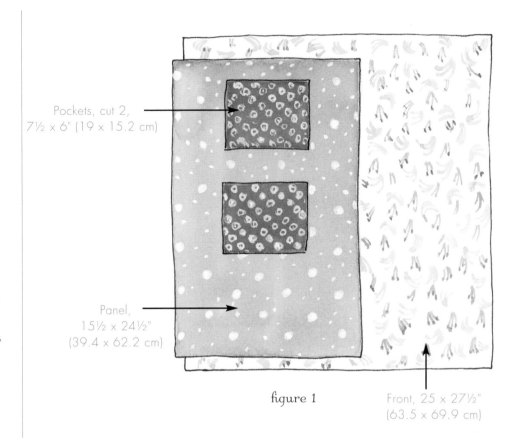

Pockets, cut 2,
7½ x 6" (19 x 15.2 cm)

Panel,
15½ x 24½"
(39.4 x 62.2 cm)

figure 1

Front, 25 x 27½"
(63.5 x 69.9 cm)

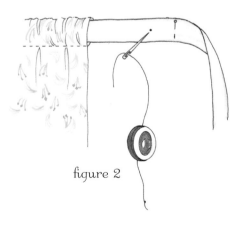

figure 2

Designer **Susan Sertain**

grape swirl

Materials

Apron kit (page 15)

Pattern (page 128)

1 yard (91.4 cm) of printed fabric for the bottom, the lining, and the yo-yo

⅜ yard (34.3 cm) of solid-colored fabric for the yoke and pocket

1 button

What You Do

1 Cut out the smock pieces using the pattern on page 128.

2 With the right sides together, sew the two yoke pieces together at the shoulders. Press the seams open. Repeat to sew the two yoke lining pieces together.

3 With the right sides together, sew the yoke lining to the yoke at the neck edge, using a ½-inch (1.3 cm) seam (figure 1). Don't trim the seam, but make small clips at the corners. Turn the yoke right side out and press, then turn it inside out again.

4 To get a clean finish at the armholes, match the armhole edges of the yoke and yoke lining on one side, with the right sides together. Stitch a ½-inch (1.3 cm) seam but don't trim it. Turn the yoke right side out, then press. Repeat to sew the other armhole.

5 Stitch the bottom pieces together at the side seams, right sides together. Gather them evenly along the top. Sew the bottom to the yoke with the right sides together, leaving a seam allowance at the armhole.

"Whenever I see vintage aprons, I think of my grandmother coming in from church and putting on her apron so she wouldn't get flour on her good dress... she made the best biscuits."
— Susan Sertain

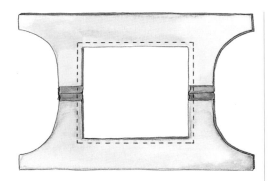

figure 1

6 Attach each armhole facing piece to each armhole of the yoke. With the right sides together, tack down the facing on the seam of the bottom.

7 Pin the armhole lining down over the gathered edge of the bottom, and then hand stitch or pin them together. On the right side of the fabric, stitch in the ditch, with the needle in the seam made while sewing the bottom to the yoke.

8 Topstitch along the bottom edge of the yoke, using a fancy machine-embroidered design.

9 To make the pocket, turn the edge under all the way around and finish by topstitching or pressing. Fold in the pleats. Create the pocket band by cutting a rectangle 5½ x 7½ inches (14 x 19 cm). Fold it in half lengthwise and match the non-folded side with the top edge of the pocket, leaving a seam allowance on each end of the band. Press the seam up. Fold the band in half toward the right side of the pocket and sew the ends. Trim the seams. Turn the band right side out and stitch to the inside. Pin the pocket to the smock and topstitch it.

10 Cut a circle of fabric with a diameter of 3½ inches (8.9 cm) and make a yo-yo from it (page 20). Stitch the yo-yo and the button to the top center of the pocket. Add any other embellishments as desired, and congratulate yourself on your—ahem— grape work.

Summertime blues

Materials

Apron kit (page 15)

Pattern (pages 122–123)

1 yard (91.4 cm) of floral fabric for the apron front, sides, and bodice

¾ yard (68.6 cm) of complementary fabric for the lower hem, waistband, waist ties, neck ties, and bodice edging

½ yard (45.7 cm) of striped fabric for the upper hem

1½ yards (1.4 m) of gathered lace trim

Seam allowance:
¼ inch (6 mm)
unless otherwise noted

What You Do

1 Use the pattern (pages 122 and 123) to cut out the apron pieces. From the floral fabric, cut out the bodice (2), the waistband lining (1), and the apron front (1), and sides (2). From the complementary fabric, cut out the neck ties (2), the bodice lining (2), the waistband (1), the waist ties (2), and the lower hem front (1), and sides (2). From the striped fabric, cut out the upper hem front (1) and the sides (2).

2 Pin and stitch each bodice edging piece to each bodice. Clip the curves and press. With the right sides together, stitch the two bodice pieces together at the front center, matching the notches and creating a seam there.

3 Fold each neck tie in half lengthwise with the wrong sides together. Stitch each together, leaving one end open. Trim the seam and the corners.

4 Turn the neck ties right side out and press. Topstitch them close to the seamed edges. Baste each tie to a bodice edging.

5 With the right sides together, stitch the two bodice lining pieces to the bodice pieces—over the neck ties— leaving the lower edges open.

Reinforce the stitching at the center front seam, being careful not to catch the neck tie in the stitching. Trim the seam, and clip the curves.

6 Turn the bodice right side out and press, flattening the neck ties. Baste the raw lower edges together. Gather the lower edge between the notches, stitching through all thicknesses.

7 With the right sides together, pin the lower edge of the bodice to the upper edge of the waistband, matching the notches. Make sure the raw edges are even. Pull up the gathering stitches to fit, and then baste (figure 1, next page). Set aside.

8 Take the waistband lining, and machine stitch ⅝ inch (1.6 cm) along its lower edge. Press under the edge along the stitching (figure 2). Place the element made in step 7 on your work surface, laying it out as shown in figure 1. Pin the waistband lining to it, with the right sides together, referring to figure 2. Stitch a seam through all the thicknesses. Trim the seam, clip the curves, and press the waistband and lining from the back, pressing the seam toward the waistband.

9 Machine stitch the apron front to the upper hem front, with a ⅝-inch (1.6 cm) seam allowance and right sides together. Also stitch the apron sides to the upper hem sides. Press all the seams open. Hem the edges.

10 Fold the top and bottom edges of the lower hem (front and sides) in ¼ inch (6 mm). Press. Place the lace trim under the lower edge of the upper hem with the ruffle out. Pin the lace and the front and sides of the lower hem in place. Machine stitch the edge of the lower hem front and sides on the seam line, catching the trim as well.

figure 1

11 Stitch the apron front to the sides, matching the upper and lower hem seams.

12 With the right sides together, pin the apron front and sides to the lower edge of the waistband, matching the center point and notches (figure 3). Stitch the seam, and then trim it. Clip the curves. Press the seam toward the waistband.

13 Fold the ties in half lengthwise, with the right sides together. Stitch the seam, leaving one end open. Trim the seam and the corners.

14 Turn the ties right side out and press. Topstitch close to the seamed edges. On the outside, pin the open end of each tie to the edge of the waistband, one on each side. Baste them together.

15 Fold the waistband with the right sides together—over the ties—and stitch across the ends through all thicknesses. Trim the seam and the corners.

16 Turn the waistband right side out. On the inside, pin the pressed edge of the waistband facing over the seam, placing the pins on the outside. On the outside, stitch the waistband close to all the seams, catching in the pressed edge of the facing on the underside. Tie it on, invite a friend over for lemonade, and bask in the compliments.

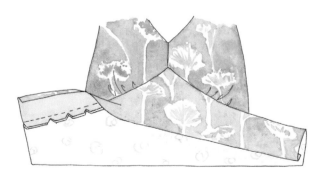

figure 2

figure 3

twirl, girl !

Materials

Apron kit (page 15)

Pattern (page 120)

1 yard (91.4 cm) of cotton fabric in a solid color

1 yard (91.4 cm) of printed cotton fabric

Tools

Quilters mat (optional)

Sewing gauge

What You Do

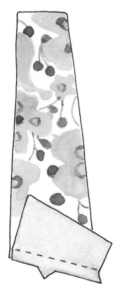

figure 1

1 Using the pattern on page 120, cut out the fabric pieces.

2 Pin one hem piece to the bottom of a front piece, right sides together and matching the notch (figure 1). Stitch a seam along the edge. Press the seams toward the hem, and topstitch close to the seam. Repeat, attaching each hem piece to a front piece.

3 Lay out one panel, right side up, and place another panel on top of it, right side down, with the edges matching. The top edge of both panels should line up as well. Pin and sew a seam along the edge. Repeat this step, connecting all the panels together. At the hem, the bottom panels should meet like the teeth of a saw (figure 2). Press the seams open, then press them all to the same side. Topstitch all the seams.

4 Make ¼-inch (6 mm) hems on both sides and at the bottom.

5 Make the waistband from the solid fabric, cutting a piece 7 x 22 inches (17.8 x 55.9 cm). Fold the waistband in half crosswise to find the center line, and mark a crease by ironing it. Find the center line of the apron, and mark it the same way.

6 Place the waistband on top of the apron front, right sides together, and line up the top edges at the crease marks. Pin. Stitch a seam along the raw edges, attaching the waistband to the front. (The extra fabric at the edges is for the seam allowances for the apron ties.)

7 Turn the apron front and waistband over, and fold the long edge of the waistband ½ inch (1.3 cm) in toward the wrong side. Press it down. Fold the waistband in half, matching up the long folded edge to the edge attached to the apron, and iron a crease.

8 To make the ties, cut two pieces of solid fabric, each 6 x 37

inches (15.2 x 94 cm). Fold each tie in half lengthwise with the right sides together and pin. Stitch a seam along the edge and one end of each tie. Trim off the seam allowances, turn the ties right side out, and press. Topstitch the edges.

9 Place the apron front and waistband right side up on your work surface. Pin one tie to one side of the waistband, matching the raw edges, close to the seam holding the front to the waistband. Repeat, pinning the other tie to the other side of the waistband.

10 Fold the waistband in half along the crease, right sides together, over the ties (figure 3). Make sure the waistband edges meet. Stitch a seam along the raw edges of the ties and waistband, sewing it in a straight line up along the sides of the waistband. Trim off the seam allowances, and turn the waistband right side out by pulling on both the apron ties.

11 With the apron facing right side down, pin the bottom of the waistband down to the seam holding the waistband to the front of the apron. Stitch a ¼-inch (6 mm) seam along the bottom edge of the waistband. Give it a final press, put it on, and twirl. It's time for a cocktail!

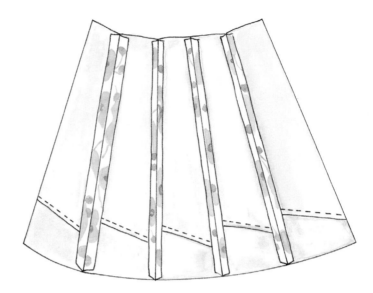

figure 2

figure 3

wash day

Materials

Apron kit (page 15)

Pattern (page 124)

1½ yards (137.2 cm) of oilcloth

½ yard (45.7 cm) of outdoor
fabric (vinyl or canvas)

Tool

Sewing machine needle designed
for sewing through thick fabrics

What You Do

1 Using the pattern on page 124, cut out the apron front from the oilcloth. Cut the pocket piece out of the outdoor fabric.

2 For the neck strap, cut out an additional piece of the outdoor fabric 2½ x 25 inches (6.4 x 63.5 cm). Then cut out two more pieces 2½ x 32 inches (6.4 x 81.3 cm) for the ties. Cut two rectangles from the oilcloth 2½ x 4 inches (6.4 x 10.2 cm).

3 Along the bottom, side, and curved edges of the apron front, fold and pin a ½-inch (1.3 cm) hem. Machine stitch the hem in place. *Note:* You should not use a hot iron on oilcloth, but you can use a cold iron or finger press seams and hems.

4 At the top of the apron front, fold the edge over 2 inches (5.1 cm), and then fold the edge in to create a 1-inch (2.5 cm) hem. Machine stitch the hem, and add a row of stitching ¼ inch (6 mm) in from the top.

5 Fold the neck strap piece and the two tie pieces in half lengthwise. Fold the edges in toward the center, and then fold the sides together. Machine stitch close to the open edge on all three pieces.

6 On the pocket piece, fold down the top edge 1 inch (2.5 cm), and machine stitch it down. Center the pocket on the apron front, and machine stitch the sides and bottom edge in place. Machine stitch down the center of the pocket, through all thicknesses, to create two pockets.

7 Position the ends of each neck strap at the top edge of the apron front on the wrong side. Overlap the straps 1 inch (2.5 cm) under the apron front. Machine stitch a rectangle around each of the strap ends. Backstitch the edge at the top of the apron front for extra hold.

8 Place the ties in position on each side of the apron front, 1 inch (2.5 cm) in from the edge. Stitch a rectangle around each tie end. Backstitch the edge closest to the side.

9 To give more strength to the edge, fold the long edges of the 2½ x 4-inch (6.4 x 10.2 cm) oilcloth rectangles in ¼ inch (6 mm). Place the shorter end right sides together with the apron over where you sewed the tie, and stitch it in place. Fold the rectangle over the apron to the wrong side, covering the tie. Fold the end under, and machine stitch the three open edges closed (figure 1).

figure 1

kaleidoscope

Designer Angelina Williamson

Materials

Apron kit (page 15)

Pattern (page 137)

¾ yard (68.6 cm) of fabric for the front

¾ yard (68.6 cm) of coordinating fabric for the waistband, hem, and ties

¼ yard (22.9 cm) of batiste for the waistband lining

4 buttons (with holes, not shanks), ⅞-inch (2.2 cm) in diameter

Tools

Spaghetti-strap turner

Seam gauge

What You Do

1 Enlarge and cut out the pattern pieces on page 137. Cut the front out of the main fabric and the remaining pattern pieces out of the coordinating fabric. Cut the waistband out of the batiste.

2 Overlock, serge, or zigzag all the raw edges of the front and hem pieces to prevent them from fraying.

3 With right sides together, pin the hem to the front, starting from the center and working toward the edges to ensure the edges match up correctly. Stitch.

4 Press the seam toward the hem, and then topstitch the seam down on the right side of the fabric.

5 Turn to the wrong side. Press and stitch down the sides.

6 Turn back to the right side, press the hem, and stitch it down.

7 Turn the four tie pieces over, wrong side up, and press one end of each, so the right side is turned over to the wrong side.

" I used pin-tucks to confer the formality of an obi or a corset. It was exciting to discover their value as both a structural and a textural element. "

—Angelina Williamson

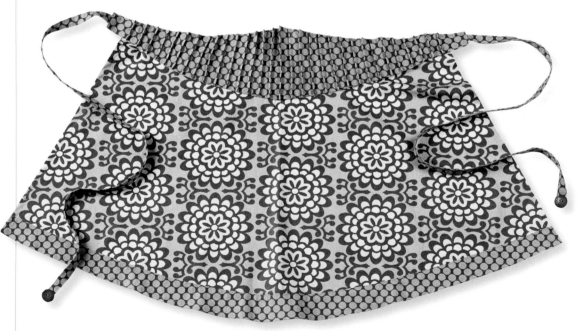

107

8 Pin two ties together, right sides together, and stitch the sides using a ¼-inch (6 mm) seam allowance. Repeat to create the other tie.

9 Turn the ties right side out using the spaghetti-strap turner, and press them. Topstitch three sides, leaving the raw edge unstitched.

10 With the right sides together, pin the waistband to the waistband lining. Stitch the sides, using a ¼-inch (6 mm) seam allowance. Turn the waistband right side out and press.

11 Turn in the ends of the waistband ½ inch (1.3 cm) and press. Insert the raw end of each apron strap into the ends of the waistband. Pin them in place, and topstitch the entire waistband.

12 Use a temporary-ink fabric pen to mark the center of the waistband at the top and the bottom. On one side of the center, use the seam gauge to make 15 small marks at the top and the bottom edges of the waistband at 1¼-inch (3.2 cm) intervals, starting from the center and working your way out. Repeat on the other side of the center mark.

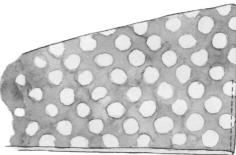

figure 1

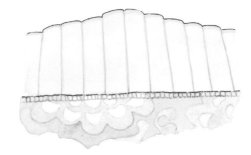

figure 2

13 Fold the waistband at the center, wrong sides together. Stitch a seam ¼ inch (6 mm) in from the center fold. Work from the center out toward one end (figure 1), and then turn the waistband around, and repeat to finish the other end. Refer to the marks you made to fold each tuck at the right spot. Stitch ¼ inch (6 mm) in from the fold each time.

14 Using a temporary-ink fabric pen, mark the center of the waistband by measuring its longest vertical length and dividing that number in half. Pin the front of the apron to the point you've marked. Then pin the rest of the front to the waistband, keeping it centered along the waistband (figure 2).

15 Use an uneven slipstitch to sew the apron front to the waistband.

16 Sandwich the end of each apron tie between two buttons, and stitch the buttons to each other. Put it on and go out for ice cream. You'll look as cool as you feel.

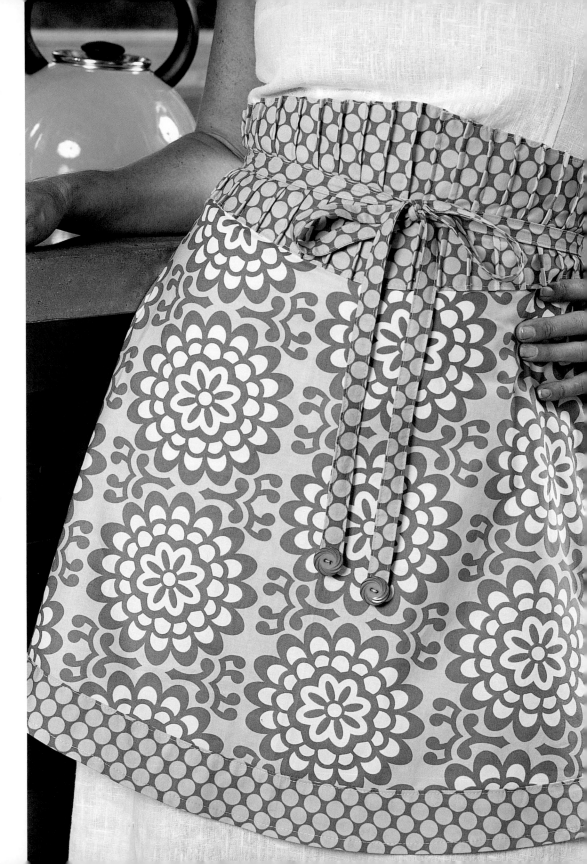

embellished
projects!

Designer Amy Tyree

dot 'em bottom

What You Need

Apron kit (page 15)

Corduroy scraps in different colors

Paper-backed fusible web

Washcloth or towel

Embroidery thread in colors matching the corduroy scraps

How You Make It

1 Iron the fusible web to the back side of the scrap corduroy using a dry iron.

2 Using random circular objects in three different sizes—a soda can, candle, and jar, for example—trace between two and five circles on each color of corduroy, drawing on the fusible's paper. Cut out the circles, and peel away the paper.

3 Place the circles on the apron, arranging them in a random, overlapping pattern. Set the iron to steam, and place the damp washcloth or towel over the apron. Press firmly until the towel is dry. Allow the apron to dry completely.

4 Put embroidery thread in the machine. Using satin stitch, sew around each circle to cover up the edges and prevent fraying, giving the circles a finished look. Trim excess threads.

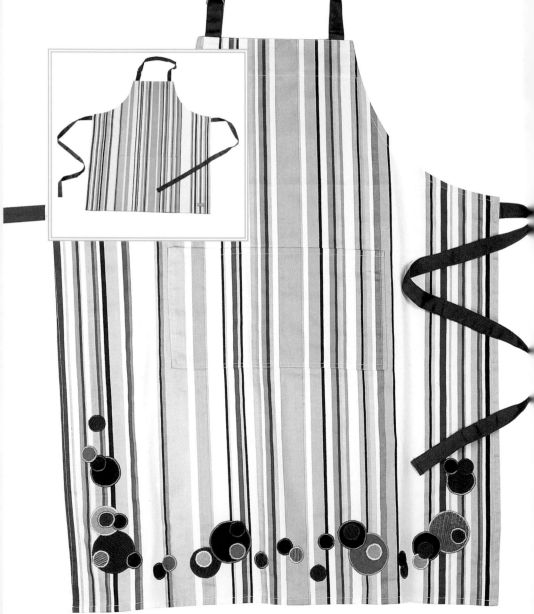

Designer **Suzanne J.E. Tourtillott**

great vine

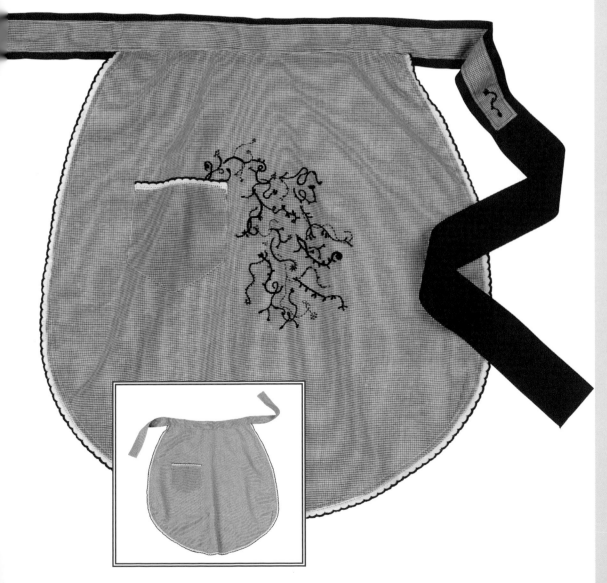

What You Need

Apron kit (page 15)

Vintage apron

Baste-on fabric stabilizer

Sharp scissors

4- or 6-inch (10.2 or 15.2 cm) embroidery hoop

1 skein of black cotton six-ply embroidery thread

Small embroidery needle

1 yard (91.4 cm) of grosgrain ribbon, 1 inch (2.5 cm) wide

Thread to match

How You Make It

1 Since soft, oft-washed fabric won't stay taut in an embroidery hoop, cut a piece of fabric stabilizer large enough to cover the design area. Baste it to the back of the apron. Position the hoop where you plan to start.

2 Embroider a free-form design with a pair of plies pulled from an 18-inch (45.7 cm) length of embroidery thread.

3 Cut the length of the grosgrain in half. Baste the ribbons to the waistband. To get the look shown here, you can first trim, turn under, and finish the ends of longer original ties. Use matching thread to topstitch the ribbon to the apron. Embroider a design on the end of the waistband.

peekaboo

What You Need

Apron kit (page 15)

Boring vintage apron

Lace curtain with interesting motif

How You Make It

1 Cut four oval shapes from the curtain.

2 Pin them evenly across the apron in a line parallel and close to the bottom.

3 Sew the ovals onto the apron with a machine, stitching around the circumference twice.

4 Turn the apron over and carefully cut out the fabric from behind the oval shapes, making sure not to snip the lace.

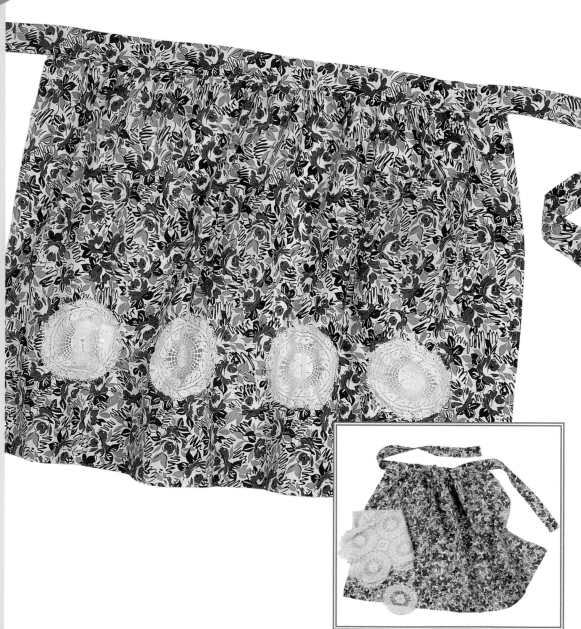

Designer **Nathalie Mornu**

skirt the issue

What You Need

Apron kit (page 15)

An old skirt

9 inches (22.9 cm) of complementary fabric

How You Make It

1 Cut the skirt along the side seams and retain the front half. Hem both sides of it. Hem the bottom shorter if you wish.

2 Cut the complementary fabric into three strips lengthwise, so that you end up with three bands 3 inches (7.6 cm) wide.

3 Sew two of the bands together along the short edge, right sides together. Use this strip to make a waist-band for the apron.

4 Cut the remaining band of comple-mentary fabric in half down its length. Stitch both pieces together along the short edge, with right sides together. Sew basting stitch-es down the center, and gather evenly and tightly to make a ruf-fle. Pin the ruffle to the bottom above the hemline; topstitch along the center of the ruffle to attach it to the apron.

Designer **Teresa Harrison Johnson**

teatime

What You Need

Apron kit (page 15)

1 long, narrow tea towel

60 inches (1.5 m) of grosgrain ribbon

1 oval doily with eyelet decoration

Lace, twice the width of the tea towel

How You Make It

1 Cut the tea towel in half widthwise. Remove the hem from the right edge of one piece and the left edge of the other. Stitch the two halves, right sides together, along the unhemmed edges.

2 Fold over the top edge ¼ inch (6 mm) toward the front of the apron. Sew a basting stitch to hold the fold. Holding one end of the basting thread, slightly gather the fabric, then knot the thread.

3 Pin the ribbon evenly across the top to form the band and apron strings, and stitch it down.

4 Cut the top third off of the oval doily. Fold under the cut edge ¼ inch (6 mm), and stitch to hem it. Sew the doily onto the apron to form a pocket.

5 Stitch the lace to the bottom of the apron.

carnival

What You Need

Apron kit (page 15)

Plain half apron

Different types of trim

How You Make It

1 Determine where you want to position the trims on the apron by spreading them out on it and playing around with the placement. In this case, the designer used 14 different types of rickrack and ribbon, spaced about ½ inch (1.3 cm) apart. If you prefer, go with a more minimalist approach—stitch on only five rows of trim just above the hem, for example.

2 Measure across the apron where you wish to sew on a particular trim. Add 1 inch (2.5 cm) to that measurement, and cut that length of trim. Repeat for each trim.

3 Pin the trims to the front of the apron, centering them and turning the extra ½ inch (1.3 cm) on each side to the back to hide the raw edges. Topstitch. You can zigzag or straight stitch down the middle, or sew along both edges of the trim.

Templates

Lemon Meringue, page 47

Enlarge 400%

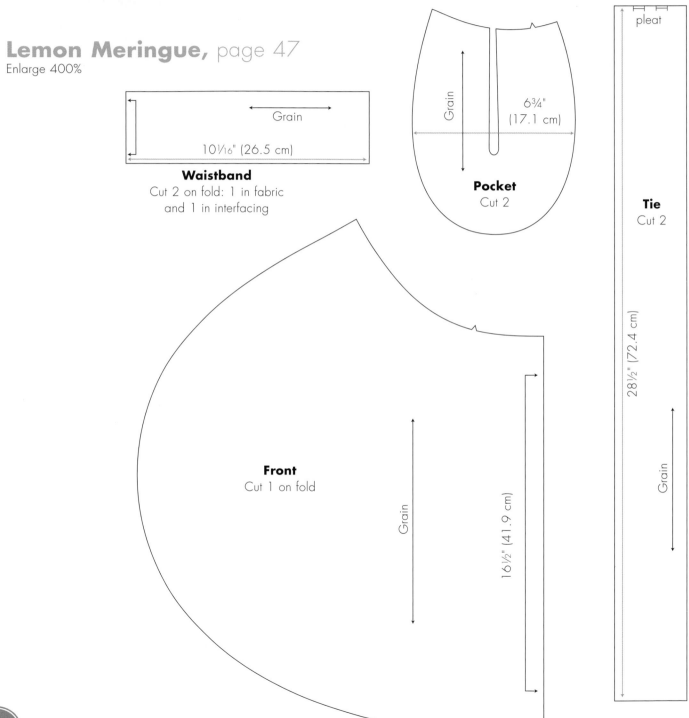

Waistband
Cut 2 on fold: 1 in fabric
and 1 in interfacing

Grain

10 1⁄16" (26.5 cm)

Grain

6¾"
(17.1 cm)

Pocket
Cut 2

Grain

Tie
Cut 2

28½" (72.4 cm)

Grain

pleat

Front
Cut 1 on fold

Grain

16½" (41.9 cm)

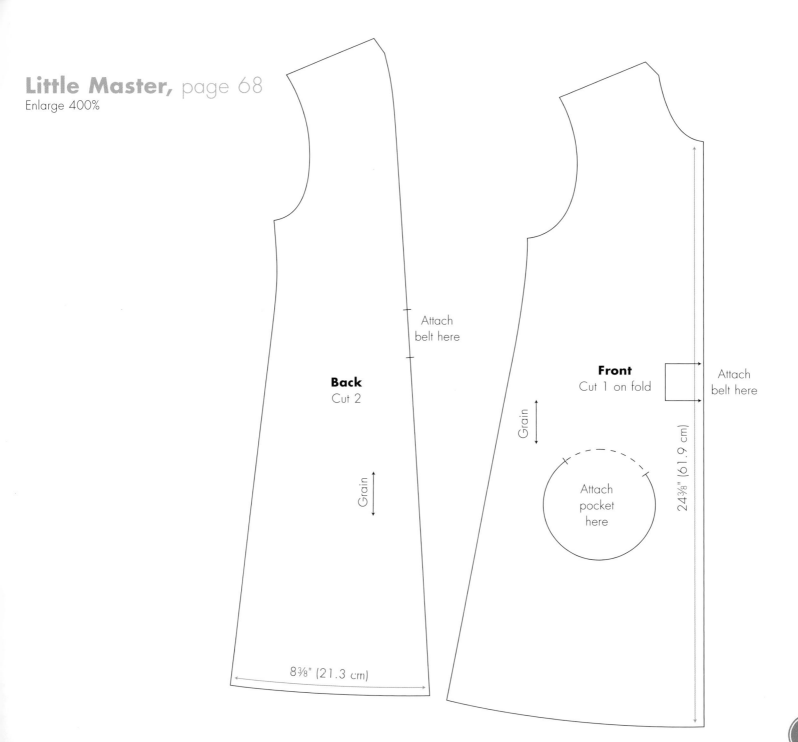

Little Master, page 68
Enlarge 400%

Attach
belt here

Back
Cut 2

Grain

8⅜" (21.3 cm)

Front
Cut 1 on fold

Attach
belt here

Grain

Attach
pocket
here

24⅜" (61.9 cm)

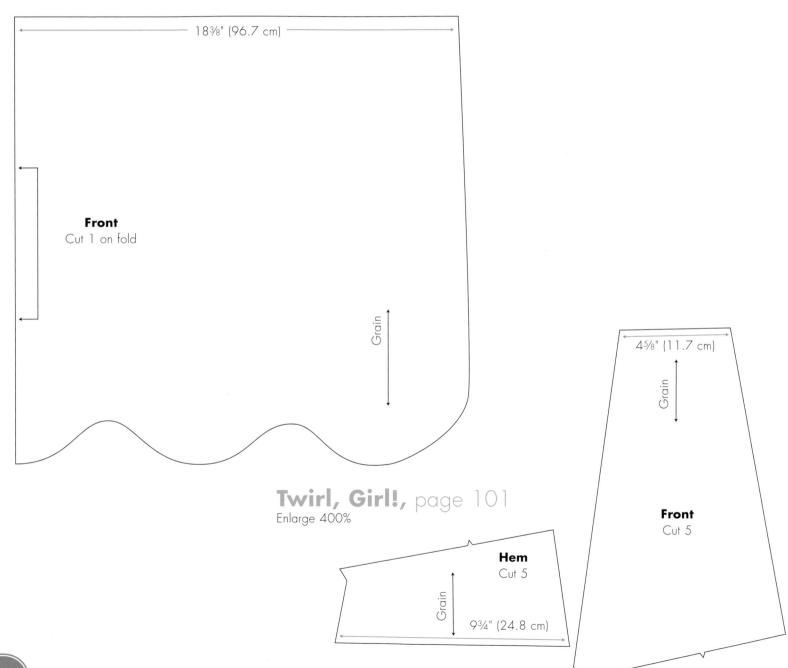

The Waldorf, page 58
Enlarge 400%

18⅜" (96.7 cm)

Front
Cut 1 on fold

Grain

Twirl, Girl!, page 101
Enlarge 400%

4⅝" (11.7 cm)

Grain

Front
Cut 5

Hem
Cut 5

Grain

9¾" (24.8 cm)

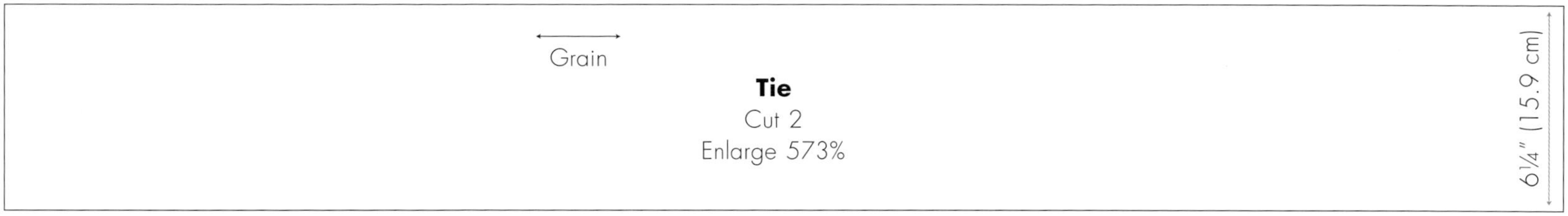

Tie
Cut 2
Enlarge 573%

Grain

6¼" (15.9 cm)

Cherry Bistro, page 42

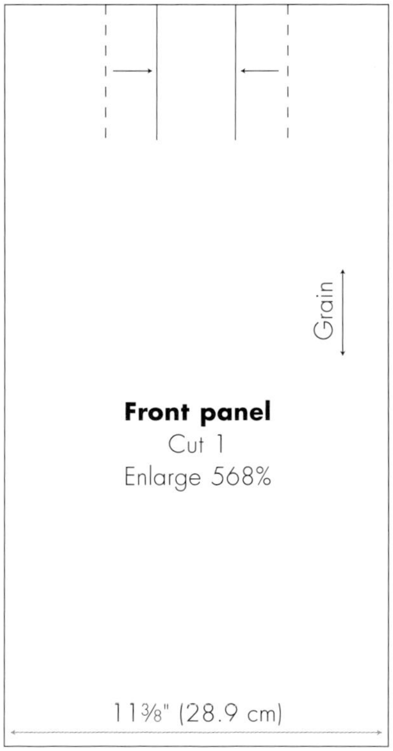

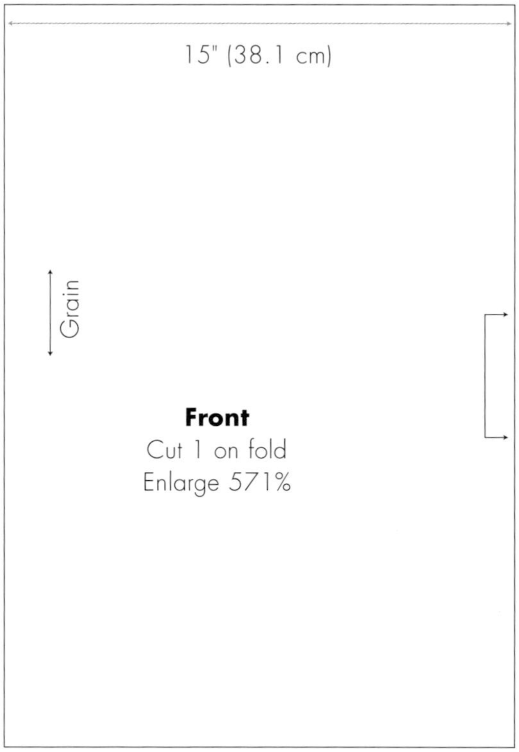

Waistband
Cut 1
Enlarge 568%

Front panel
Cut 1
Enlarge 568%

Grain

11⅜" (28.9 cm)

15" (38.1 cm)

Front
Cut 1 on fold
Enlarge 571%

Grain

Grain

6¼"
(15.9 cm)

Summertime Blues, page 98

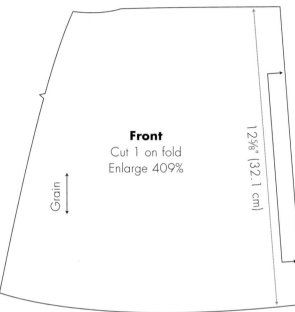

Front
Cut 1 on fold
Enlarge 409%

Grain

12⅝" (32.1 cm)

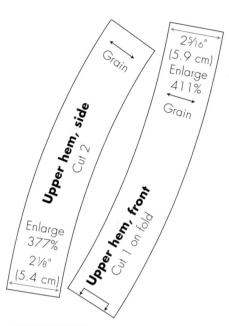

Grain

2⁵⁄₁₆"
(5.9 cm)
Enlarge
411%

Grain

Upper hem, side
Cut 2

Enlarge
377%
2⅛"
(5.4 cm)

Upper hem, front
Cut 1 on fold

3¼" (8.3 cm)

Grain

Neck tie
Cut 2
Enlarge 400%

Side
Cut 2
Enlarge 404%

11⅝" (29.5 cm)

Grain

Tie
Cut 2
Enlarge 400%

27¾" (70.5 cm)

Grain

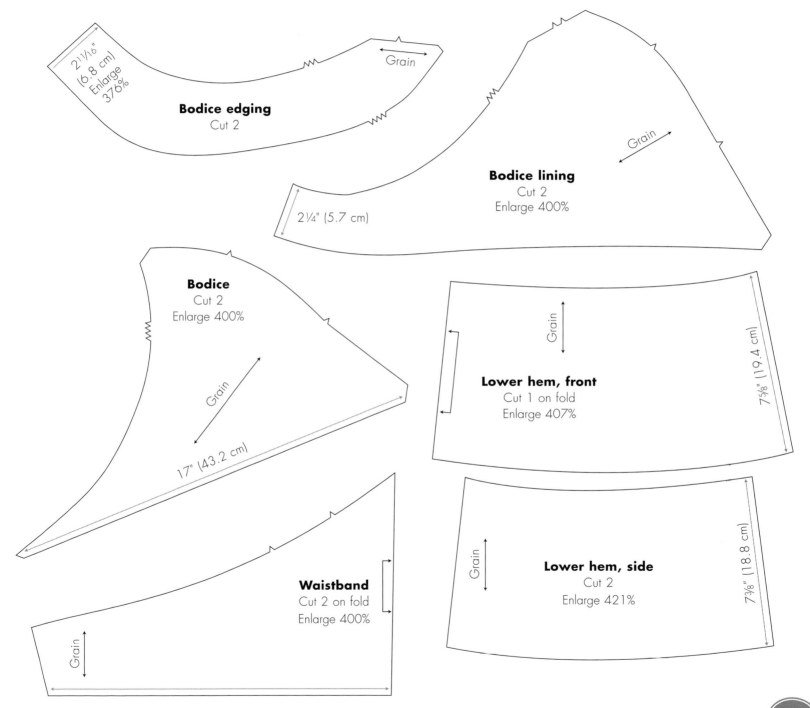

Bodice edging
Cut 2

2 11/16"
(6.8 cm)
Enlarge
376%

Grain

Bodice lining
Cut 2
Enlarge 400%

Grain

2¼" (5.7 cm)

Bodice
Cut 2
Enlarge 400%

Grain

17" (43.2 cm)

Lower hem, front
Cut 1 on fold
Enlarge 407%

Grain

7⅝" (19.4 cm)

Waistband
Cut 2 on fold
Enlarge 400%

Grain

Lower hem, side
Cut 2
Enlarge 421%

Grain

7⅜" (18.8 cm)

Wash Day, page 104
Enlarge 579%

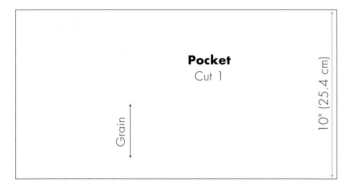

Pocket
Cut 1

Grain

10" (25.4 cm)

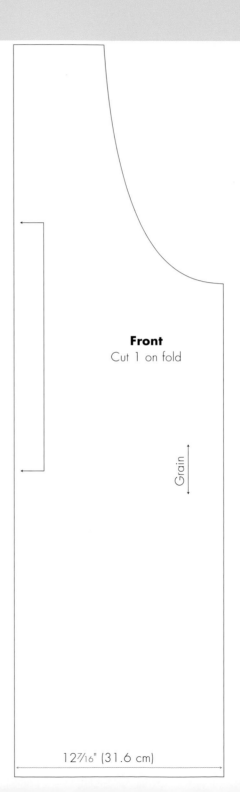

Front
Cut 1 on fold

Grain

12⁷⁄₁₆" (31.6 cm)

Pop Beads, page 88

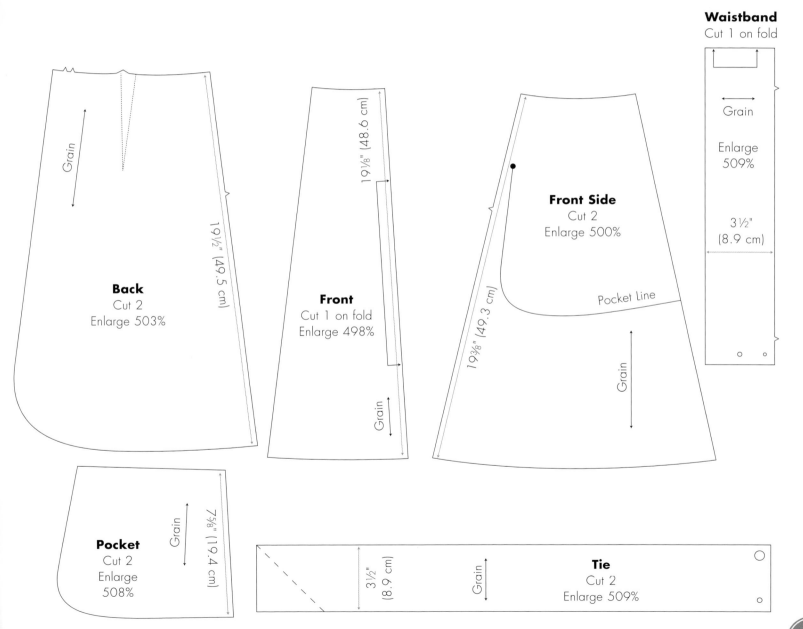

Waistband
Cut 1 on fold

Grain

Enlarge
509%

3½"
(8.9 cm)

Grain

19⅛" (48.6 cm)

Front
Cut 1 on fold
Enlarge 498%

Grain

Back
Cut 2
Enlarge 503%

Grain

19½" (49.5 cm)

Front Side
Cut 2
Enlarge 500%

19⅜" (49.3 cm)

Pocket Line

Grain

Pocket
Cut 2
Enlarge
508%

Grain

7⅝" (19.4 cm)

3½"
(8.9 cm)

Grain

Tie
Cut 2
Enlarge 509%

Fruit Tart, page 52

Enlarge 400%

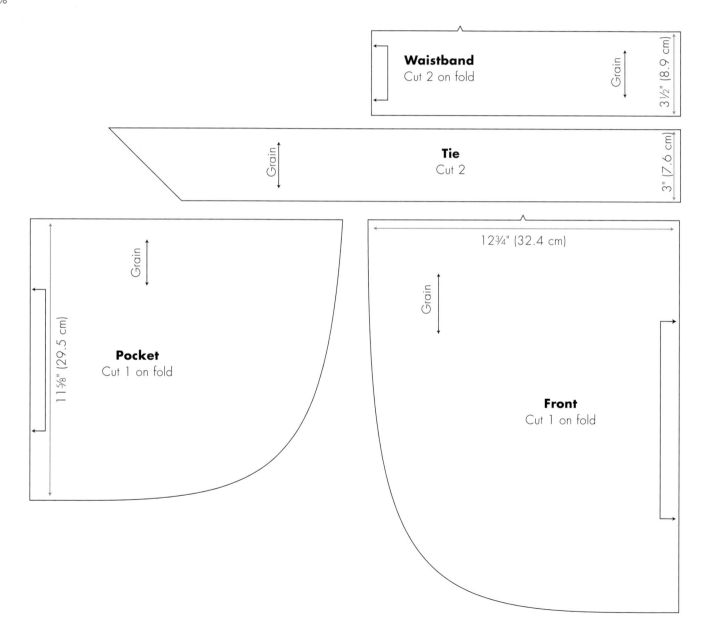

Waistband
Cut 2 on fold

Grain

3½" (8.9 cm)

Grain

Tie
Cut 2

3" (7.6 cm)

Grain

Pocket
Cut 1 on fold

11⅝" (29.5 cm)

12¾" (32.4 cm)

Grain

Front
Cut 1 on fold

Fairy Tale, page 50

Enlarge 200%

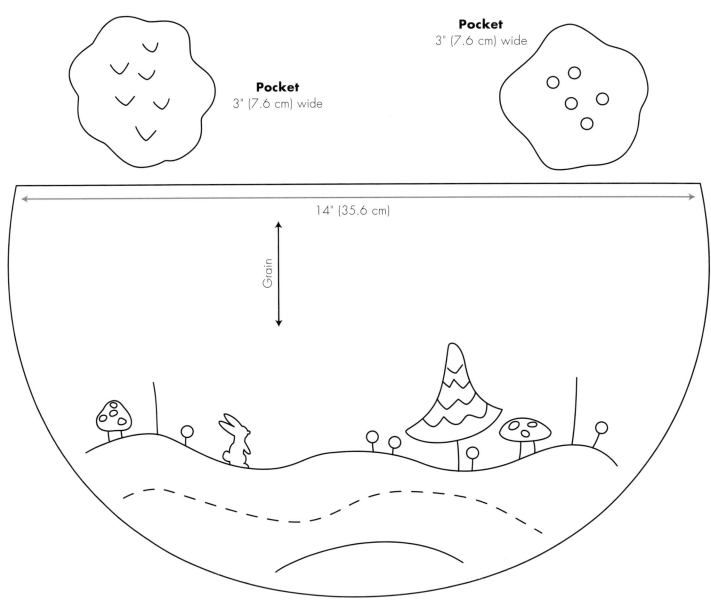

Pocket
3" (7.6 cm) wide

Pocket
3" (7.6 cm) wide

14" (35.6 cm)

Grain

Grape Swirl, page 96

Enlarge 400%

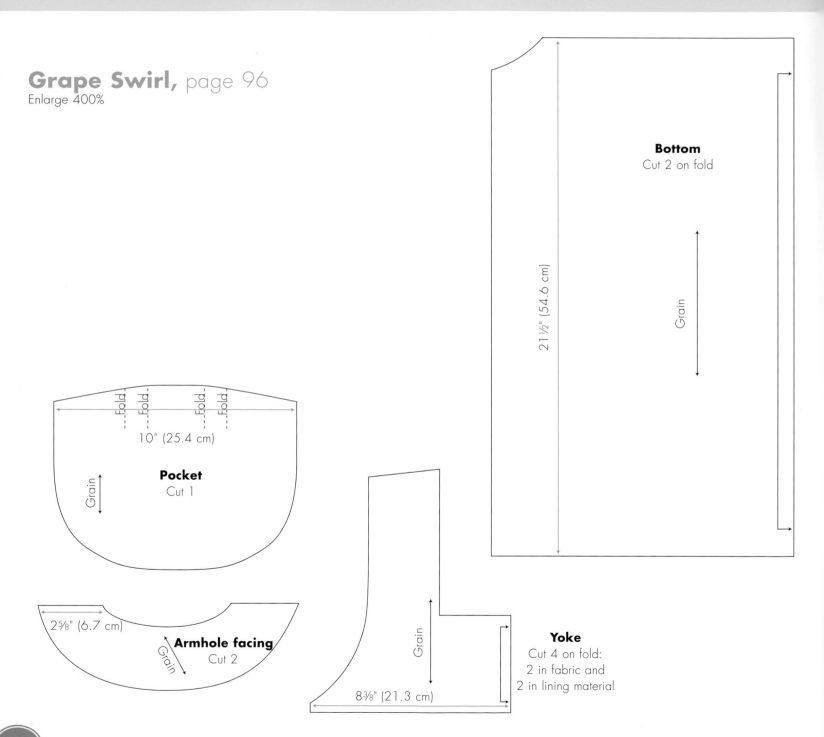

Bottom
Cut 2 on fold

21½" (54.6 cm)

Grain

Pocket
Cut 1

10" (25.4 cm)

Fold Fold Fold Fold

Grain

2⅝" (6.7 cm)

Armhole facing
Cut 2

Grain

Grain

Yoke
Cut 4 on fold:
2 in fabric and
2 in lining material

8⅜" (21.3 cm)

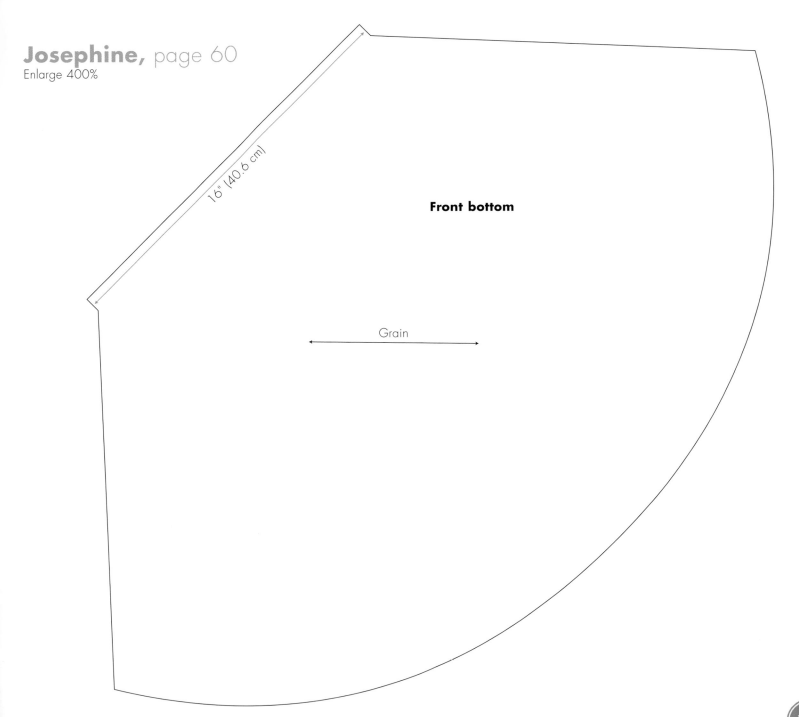

Josephine, page 60
Enlarge 400%

1'6" (40.6 cm)

Front bottom

Grain

Marie Antoinette, page 84

Enlarge 400%

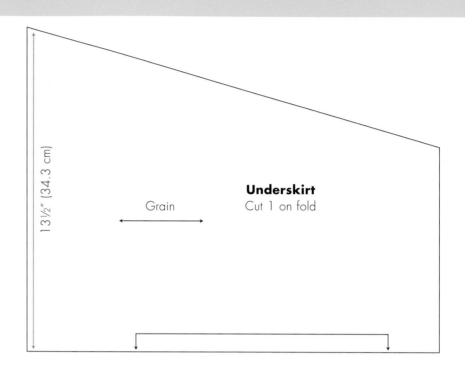

Underskirt
Cut 1 on fold

Grain

13½" (34.3 cm)

Deep Pockets, page 55

Enlarge 400%

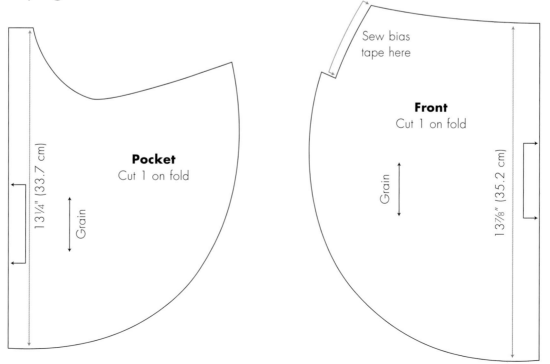

Pocket
Cut 1 on fold

13¼" (33.7 cm)

Grain

Sew bias tape here

Front
Cut 1 on fold

Grain

13⅞" (35.2 cm)

Psychedelic Squares, page 90

Enlarge 450%

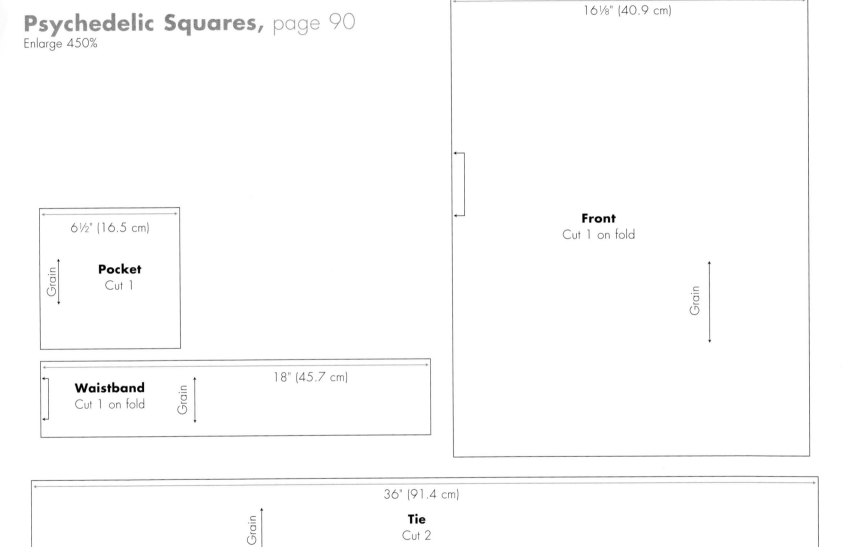

6½" (16.5 cm)

Grain

Pocket
Cut 1

18" (45.7 cm)

Grain

Waistband
Cut 1 on fold

16⅛" (40.9 cm)

Front
Cut 1 on fold

Grain

36" (91.4 cm)

Grain

Tie
Cut 2

Provence Smock, page 76

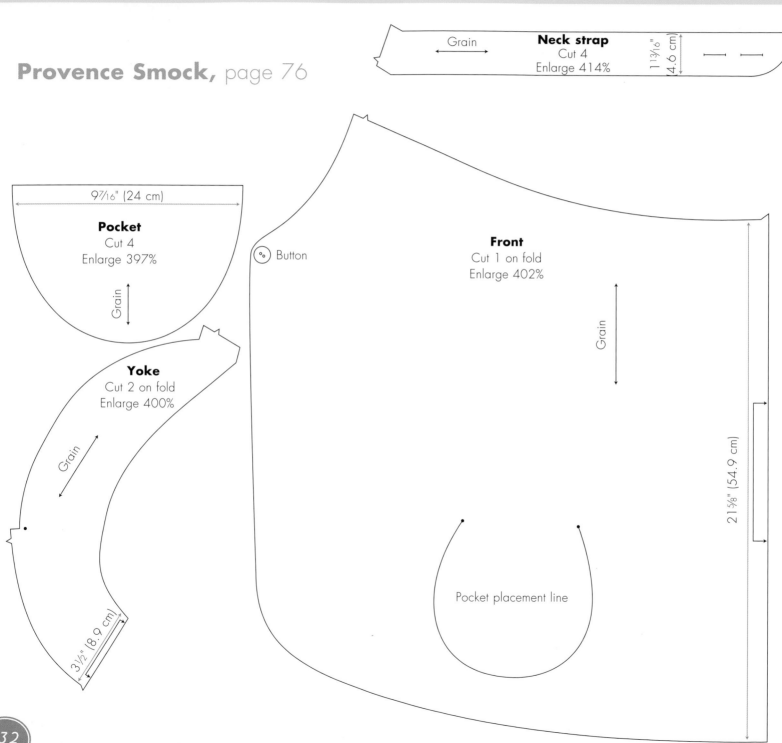

Neck strap
Cut 4
Enlarge 414%

Grain

1 13/16" (4.6 cm)

9 7/16" (24 cm)

Pocket
Cut 4
Enlarge 397%

Grain

Button

Front
Cut 1 on fold
Enlarge 402%

Grain

21 5/8" (54.9 cm)

Yoke
Cut 2 on fold
Enlarge 400%

Grain

3 1/2" (8.9 cm)

Pocket placement line

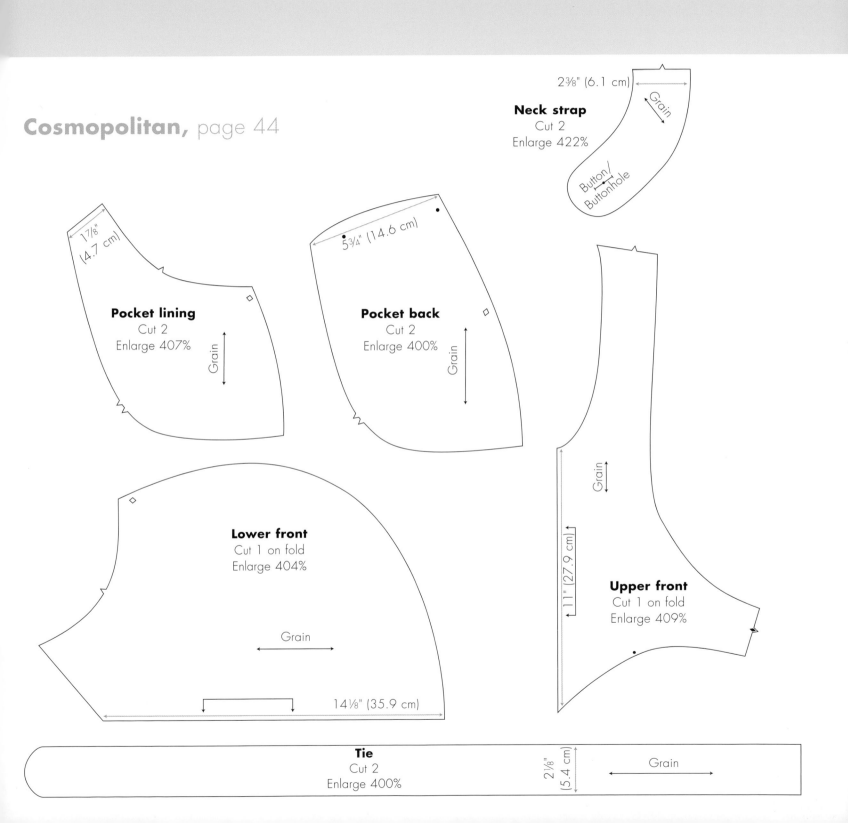

Cosmopolitan, page 44

Neck strap
Cut 2
Enlarge 422%

2⅜" (6.1 cm)

Grain

Button /
Buttonhole

1⅞"
(4.7 cm)

Pocket lining
Cut 2
Enlarge 407%

Grain

5¾" (14.6 cm)

Pocket back
Cut 2
Enlarge 400%

Grain

Grain

11" (27.9 cm)

Upper front
Cut 1 on fold
Enlarge 409%

Lower front
Cut 1 on fold
Enlarge 404%

Grain

14⅛" (35.9 cm)

Tie
Cut 2
Enlarge 400%

2⅛"
(5.4 cm)

Grain

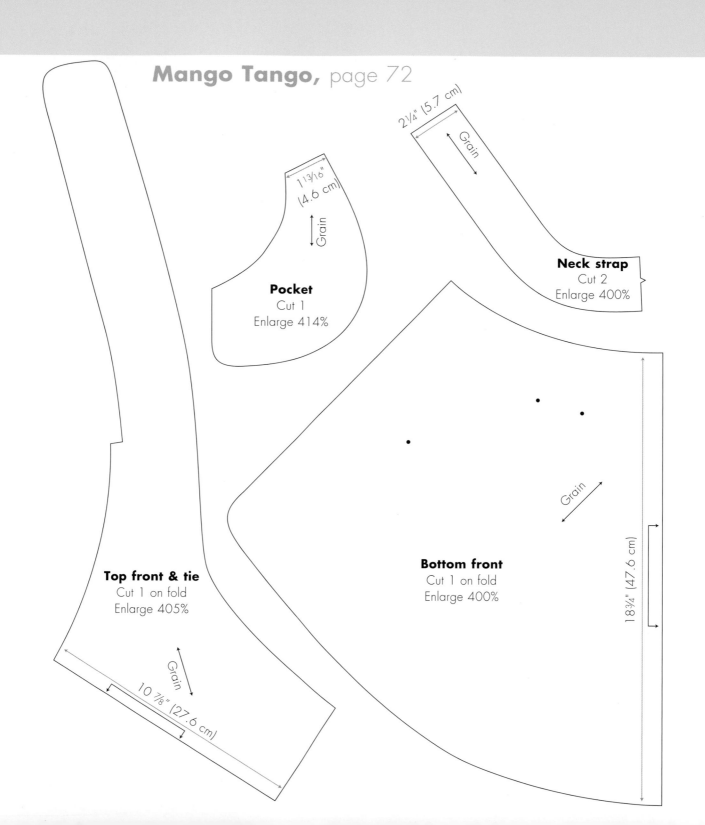

Mango Tango, page 72

2¼" (5.7 cm)

Grain

1¹³/₁₆"
(4.6 cm)

Grain

Pocket
Cut 1
Enlarge 414%

Neck strap
Cut 2
Enlarge 400%

Top front & tie
Cut 1 on fold
Enlarge 405%

Grain

10 ⅞" (27.6 cm)

Bottom front
Cut 1 on fold
Enlarge 400%

Grain

18¾" (47.6 cm)

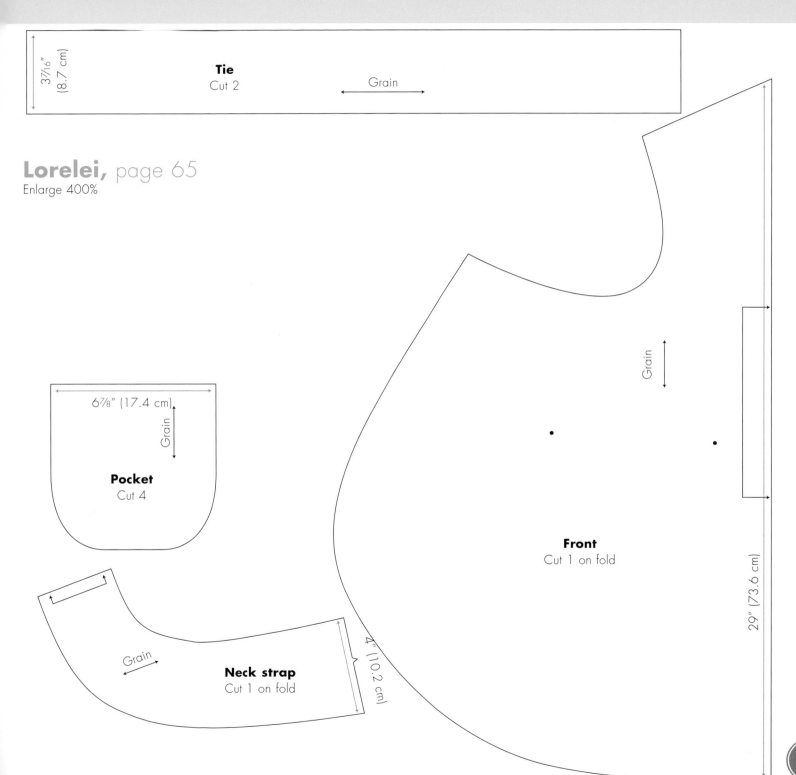

Tie
Cut 2

Grain

3⁷⁄₁₆" (8.7 cm)

Lorelei, page 65
Enlarge 400%

6⁷⁄₈" (17.4 cm)

Grain

Pocket
Cut 4

Grain

Neck strap
Cut 1 on fold

4" (10.2 cm)

Grain

Front
Cut 1 on fold

29" (73.6 cm)

Amoeba, page 34

Enlarge 400%

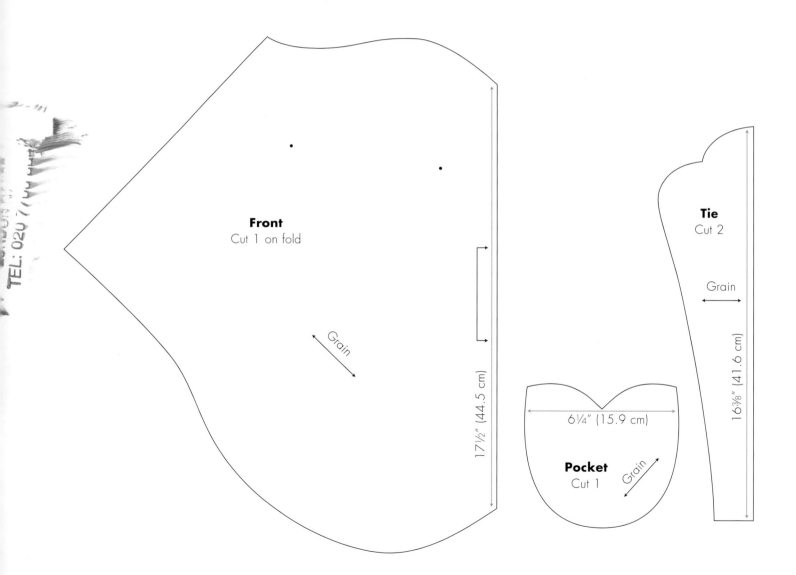

Front
Cut 1 on fold

Grain

17½" (44.5 cm)

6¼" (15.9 cm)

Pocket
Cut 1

Grain

Tie
Cut 2

Grain

16⅜" (41.6 cm)

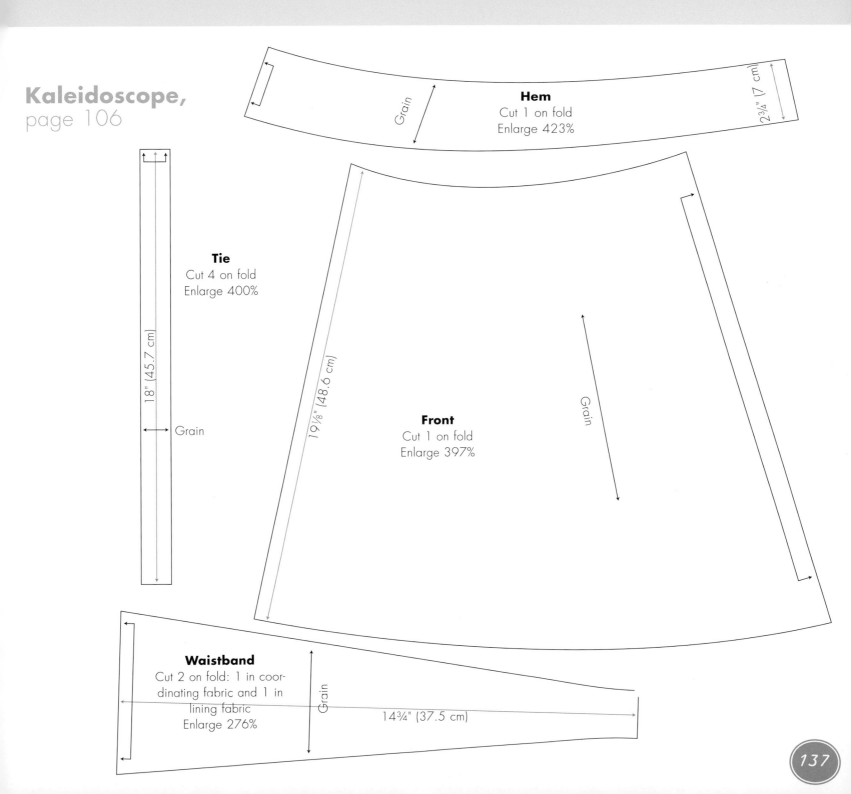

Kaleidoscope,
page 106

Hem
Cut 1 on fold
Enlarge 423%

Grain

2¾" (7 cm)

Tie
Cut 4 on fold
Enlarge 400%

18" (45.7 cm)

Grain

Front
Cut 1 on fold
Enlarge 397%

19⅛" (48.6 cm)

Grain

Waistband
Cut 2 on fold: 1 in coor-
dinating fabric and 1 in
lining fabric
Enlarge 276%

Grain

14¾" (37.5 cm)

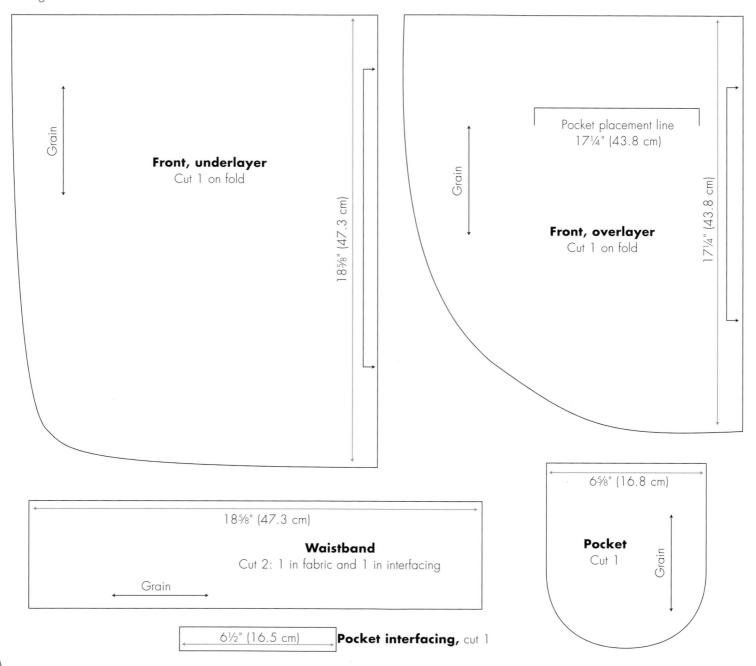

Cakeland, page 40

Enlarge 400%

Grain

Front, underlayer
Cut 1 on fold

18⅝" (47.3 cm)

Pocket placement line
17¼" (43.8 cm)

Grain

Front, overlayer
Cut 1 on fold

17¼" (43.8 cm)

18⅝" (47.3 cm)

Waistband
Cut 2: 1 in fabric and 1 in interfacing

Grain

6⅝" (16.8 cm)

Pocket
Cut 1

Grain

6½" (16.5 cm) **Pocket interfacing,** cut 1

About the Designers

Betsy Couzins has worked as a mixed-media artist since her pilgrim diorama project received an "A" in the second grade. Her work has been featured in two other Lark books: *Altered Art* by Terry Taylor (2004) and *The Decorated Journal* by Gwen Diehn (2005). Her creations have also graced the pages of several national periodicals, including *Jane* and *Artitude*. Betsy currently resides in Asheville, North Carolina, with her husband and son. Her blog, located at wonderland5.typepad.com, chronicles her increasing love of working with fabric.

Wendi Gratz lives with her family and her sewing machine just down the road from the Penland School of Crafts in western North Carolina. In high school, she skipped home economics in favor of wood and metal shop, so she didn't learn to use a sewing machine until she was in college. Her first sewing project was a badly made tablecloth. Wendi learned a lot from that disastrous endeavor; her second project was designing and making all the costumes for a play. Now she makes fun clothes, funky dolls, and all kinds of quilts. You can see her work at www.wendigratz.com.

As a young child, **Erin Harris** made things like woven potholders and plastic canvas embroideries. She learned to sew in junior high school and didn't stop there. Now she knits, crochets, and embroiders, although sewing is still her real love. She and her family live in Louisville, Kentucky, where Erin always keeps a project or two going whenever she's not chasing children or driving carpools. Her daughters are the primary recipients of her handcrafted goodies. She recounts her adventures in craft on her website, www.houseonhillroad.com.

designer
Erin Harris

Teresa Harrison Johnson is currently fending off empty-nest syndrome by remodeling her home, managing a meal-site sponsored by her local Council on Aging, crafting puzzle boards, pet sitting, doing accounting work, and embellishing aprons. Despite this list of activities, she's not overwhelmed. She defines herself as a person who likes creating things, being helpful, and staying busy with a variety of different projects.

Samantha Kramer tends to her son and to her business, Homegrown Skinny Handmade Goods (homegrownskinny.etsy.com). In her spare time, she dreams of going thrifting again. A proud member of the MTV generation, she credits her family for their inspiration and encouragement, and thanks her Great-Granny for supplying "all that rad vintage fabric" that started her off. Learn more about Sam by visiting her blog at homegrownskinny.wordpress.com, where you can read about her sewing exploits, her love of trees, and the music she digs. Her store sells hip bags, retro pillows, and the occasional vintage-inspired apron.

On most days, you'll find designer **Morgan Moore** whipping up delicious treats in her kitchen or designing new products for her online shop—all while chasing around a two-year-old toddler. Besides being a mother, she's also an artist and self-described fabric junkie. Morgan loves to sew and thinks aprons are the hippest things around. Based in Los Angeles, California, she lives with her husband and son. Visit her on her blog, "One More Moore," at morganmoore.typepad.com.

Joan K. Morris's artistic endeavors have led her down many successful, creative paths, including ceramics and costume design for motion pictures. Joan has contributed projects to numerous Lark books, including *Cutting Edge Decoupage* (2007), *Creative Stitching on Paper* (2006), *Exquisite Embellishments for Your Clothes* (2006), *Hip Handbags* (2005), *Gifts For Baby* (2004), *Hardware Style* (2004), and *Beautiful Ribbon Crafts* (2003).

Jennifer M. Ramos fondly remembers that giant stuffed pencil she made in seventh grade, and admiring her mother's green Kenmore sewing machine but not being allowed to touch it. More recently, Jennifer started a home-based business—Textile Fetish (www.textilefetish.com)—that sells one-of-a-kind handmade items made mostly from reclaimed and recycled materials. "The act of acquiring and recycling fabric scraps and remnants is addictive," she says. The lure of quilt shops, the treasures from thrift stores, and the fabric stashes from friends keep her sane and supplied.

Aimee Ray has been making things for as long as she can remember, and her head is still full of ideas. As a graphic designer in the greeting card and comic book industries—and with several personal projects in the works—she is never without something creative at hand. Her interests range from digital painting and illustration to sewing stuffed animals, embroidery, and everything in between. She is the author of *Doodle Stitching* (Lark Books, 2007), a book of contemporary embroidery designs and projects. You can see more of Aimee's work at her website, www.dreamfollow.com.

Susan Sertain has sewn most of her life; for the last 15 years, she has made her career as a costume maker. Working on this book stirred up all sorts of pleasant memories about her grandmother's country kitchen and delicious cooking. An avid pattern collector, Susan has several old apron patterns. She loves working with textures and movement in fabric and always looks for the chance to use a vintage button or two. After noticing vintage aprons being used in kitchen decorating—such as window treatments—Susan is glad to see them being taken seriously again, both in home decor and as fashion accessories. She lives in Asheville, North Carolina, where she owns a business named The Costume Shoppe.

Valerie Shrader made a pair of pink culottes when she was 11 and has loved fabric ever since. As a senior editor at Lark Books, she has written and edited many books related to textiles and needlework. She knits every now and then, too, and hopes that art quilts will be her next creative exploration. Recently, she celebrated her midlife crisis by purchasing three sewing machines in one year.

A British designer who works with recycled and natural fabrics, Ruth Singer creates contemporary handmade fashion and interior accessories inspired by historic textiles. She uses traditional techniques—pleating, appliqué, folding, layering, and quilting—to create the unusual textures and sculptural effects in her scarves, bags, and cushions. Her work is highly decorative and often heavily embellished. In 2006, the Crafts Council selected her as one of the best new makers of the year. Ruth recently designed a small collection of fabric corsages for an ethical fashion company. Find out about her latest projects at www.ruthsinger.com.

After careers in advertising and as a paralegal, Carrie Sommer began freelance writing and designing websites. When she made a diaper bag for a friend, her business—Sommer Designs, www.sommerdesigns.com—was redefined nearly overnight. Now she gets to indulge her obsession with color and patterns. Her new products include handmade handbags and home items. Eye-catching fabrics and crisp, traditional shapes have become her trademark, and the combinations of patterns add a touch of whimsy. Carrie lives in Southern California with her husband, three teenage sons, two silly dogs, and a shy cat.

designer
Ruth Singer

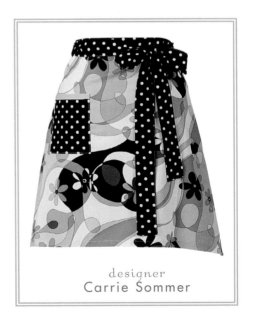

designer
Carrie Sommer

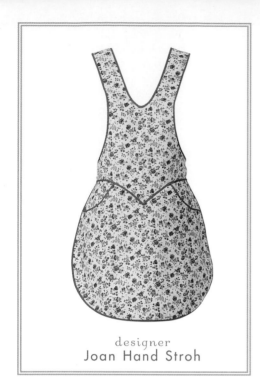

designer
Joan Hand Stroh

Joan Hand Stroh is just a gal who likes to sew. She's been at it since childhood, when her mother let her loose with a huge pair of scissors and a piece of fabric. Lately, she's been sewing and selling retro-inspired aprons. "I want my aprons to be flattering, well-made, and most of all, affordable," she says. She lives in central Texas with her husband, who patiently accompanies her on the never-ending searches for new fabrics. She credits her daughter-in-law for suggesting apron making as a pastime. You can find more aprons at her website, momomadeit.etsy.com.

Suzanne J.E. Tourtillott creates one-of-a-kind freehand embroidery designs in her spare time. Brief craft flare-ups in knitting, ink sketching, and watercolor also distract her from her job as a senior editor at Lark Books. She spends hours every week scouring fashion and indie-craft websites and publications. Former life directions include teaching college-level photography, serving fine dining and cocktails, office administration, house painting, freelance art writing, and pulling suckers in a tomato greenhouse. She is a committed Nana to three adorable granddaughters and does tons of volunteer work. What time is left remaining she spends pursuing reading, meditation, and spiritual insight.

Amy Tyree grew up in Dayton, Ohio, but lived in Red Cliff, Colorado, for many years before moving to Asheville, North Carolina. Her first love has always been art—drawing, painting, sketching, and eventually sewing. She sells one-of-a-kind wearable art and accessories under the name Amiable Creations; you can check out Amy's latest designs at her website,www.amiablecreations.com.

After years in the clothing design industry, **Angelina Williamson** found her calling developing aprons. They reflect her love of color and irreverence. "Despite their humble purpose," she says, "aprons embody the most wonderful sense of playfulness and beauty." Her design work reflects her deep respect for home arts and the quality of our lives. She loves putting on her apron to dig in the dirt or play in the kitchen. You can find Angelina through her accessories company, Dustpan Alley, at www.dustpanalley.com.

designer
Angelina Williamson

acknowledgments

This book couldn't have come together without the enthusiasm of the talented designers who contributed projects. I appreciate the passion they poured into the task.

Thank you to the lovely models who showed off the aprons to best advantage: Laurel Ashton; Martia Bennett; Megan Cooke and her little dog Joe, who narrowly avoided a washing during the photo shoot (whew!); Dawn Dickinson; Sophia Hon Fuge Ewing; Hazel Grotenhuis; Leslie Grotenhuis; Sarah Jamison; Maggie Mathena; Abby Semon; Jasmine Villarreal; and Kristen Welch. John Widman did a terrific job photographing them all.

Thank you to the homeowners who graciously allowed us to shoot inside their beautiful houses: Stephen Beili, Jo and Kevin Hogan, and Dick and Judy Warner.

Several Asheville, North Carolina, businesses also helped out. Bouchon French Bistro gave permission to take photos in their courtyard, and Waechter's Silk Shop loaned a dress form.

When you tell folks you're working on a book about aprons, aficionados come out of the woodwork immediately, eager to share their collections. I'm grateful to all the friends and colleagues who loaned the vintage aprons and pattern envelopes shown in this book: Edith Broward; Avery Johnson; Teresa Harrison Johnson; Megan Kirby; Corinne Kurzman, owner of Diggin Art in West Asheville, North Carolina—possibly the coolest vintage store anywhere; William Lishman, who loaned a score of aprons made by his late aunt, Julia Adelaide Lishman Harris; Suzie Millions, who owns loads and loads of vintage aprons; Eden Reinstein and her mother Naomi Abrams Reinstein, whose purchase of a vintage apron was inspired by a duckling hatch; Kathy Sheldon; and Terry Taylor.

The apron-wearing divas drawn by Amy Saidens add a bunch of sass to these pages. Bernadette Wolf's instructional illustrations are so pretty, they're a sheer delight. Dana Irwin pulled out all the stops in her design of the book, and the art production team of Jeff Hamilton and Avery Johnson kept the project smoothly on track. Finally, huge props to the top-notch editorial team that worked on all aspects of this book: Mark Bloom, Amanda Carestio (who also loaned her baby blue scooter for the photo shoot), Emily Chatfield, Jess Clarke, Rosemary Kast, and Kathleen McCafferty.

index